Fearless Budgeting

A Gentle, Step-by-Step Training Program for Compulsive Spenders

Susan B.

Getting Out from Going Under Publishing

Wellington, Florida

Copyright © 2018 by **Getting Out from Going Under Publishing**

All rights reserved. No part of this publication may be reproduced, distributed or transmitted in any form or by any means, without prior written permission.

Susan B./Getting Out from Going Under Publishing
14611 Southern Boulevard
Suite 101
Loxahatchee, FL 33470
www.FearlessBudgeting.wordpress.com

Fearless Budgeting/Susan B. -- 1st ed.
ISBN 978-1979850124

Dedicated to Jay
Thank you for always being there for me. You are my rock and my grounding.

Contents

PLEASE READ THIS FIRST ix

COURSE I FOUNDATIONAL COURSE: CREATING YOUR SPENDING PLAN 1

   SECTION I: BEFORE YOU BEGIN 3

      Lesson #1: Welcome 5

      Lesson #2: How to Take the Course and Additional Options 9

      Lesson #3: So Why *Do* You Need a Spending Plan? 13

      Lesson #4: Please Do Not Jump Ahead 15

      Lesson #5: Crucial Lesson Spending Plan vs. Budget 17

      Lesson #6: The Foundational Document and Meeting Delayed Gratification 21

   SECTION II: BUILDING A FOUNDATION 23

      Lesson #7: Let's Begin 25

      Lesson #8: Handouts for Building Your Foundation 27

      Lesson #9: Categories 29

      Lesson #10: Master and Subcategories 33

      Lesson #11: Special Circumstances 57

      Lesson #12: Is There a Miscellaneous Category? 65

      Lesson #13: About Your Debts 67

      Lesson #14: Small Business and Hobby Tax Reporting Made Easy 71

      Lesson #15: Next Step 77

   SECTION III: COMPLETING THE FRAMEWORK 79

      Lesson #16: Getting Ready for Deeper Water 81

      Lesson #17: It's Time to Begin Tracking Your Spending 83

      Lesson #18: Detective Work Part I 87

      Lesson #19: Detective Work Part II 97

- Lesson #20: Add Up the Numbers on the Worksheet 105
- Lesson #21: For Those with Debt 107
- Lesson #22: Time to Talk Income 113
- Lesson #23: Adding Up Your Master Categories and Income 121
- Lesson #24: Calculating Your Foundational Number 123

SECTION IV: TRANSFORMING THE FOUNDATION INTO A SPENDING PLAN 127

- Lesson #25: It's All About Choices 129
- Lesson #26: Congratulations! 137

COURSE II WORKING WITH YOUR SPENDING PLAN 139

SECTION I: BEFORE YOU BEGIN 141

- Lesson #1: Welcome 143
- Lesson #2: Components of an Effective Spending Plan 145
- Lesson #3: Options for Working with Your Spending Plan 149

SECTION II: HOW WILL YOU TRACK YOUR SPENDING? 153

- Lesson #4: How do You Get Paid? 155
- Lesson #5: Living in the Next Month 157
- Lesson #6: If You are Paid Weekly 163
- Lesson #7: More on Periodic Bills 169
- Lesson #8: Romancing Temptation 175
- Lesson #9: Keeping Track of Your Numbers 177
- Lesson #10: Automatic Withdrawals and Deposits 181
- Lesson #11: Reconciling 183
- Lesson #12: Dealing with Cash 191

SECTION III: RELATIONSHIPS AND MONEY 193

- Lesson #13: Your Partner and the Spending Plan 195
- Lesson #14: Children and Your Spending Plan 199
- Lesson #15: When Parents Give Us Money 203
- Lesson #16: Lending Money 205

    Lesson #17: Lesson Gift-Giving Tips 207

SECTION IV: BONUS TIPS 211

    Lesson #18: Moving Money Between Categories 213

    Lesson #19: Delayed Gratification 215

    Lesson #20: Dealing with Debt 217

    Lesson #21: Quick Tips Regarding Refunds and Library Books 223

    Lesson #22: Checking Accounts with Interest! 225

    Lesson #23: Overview of My Spending Plan Process 227

    Lesson #24: Congratulations and Thank You 229

RESOURCES 231

PLEASE READ THIS FIRST

YOU HOLD IN YOUR HANDS the complete Fearless Budgeting Training Program for compulsive spenders. With the help of this training program, you will finally be able to create a spending plan and learn how to integrate it into your life. Since this book was written by a recovering compulsive spender, I understand, as "normal" spenders and the financial gurus can't, the unique struggles you face and why you haven't been able to succeed at this process in the past ... and I'll help you overcome these obstacles to your success.

The spending plan is one crucial weapon in an arsenal you need to recover from compulsive spending. And that's the one we're going to address in this training program.

I developed the Fearless Budgeting Training Program based on my own experience helping many others, just like you. Through this training, you will begin to overcome feelings of shame around your spending, anxiety and fear at the thought of dealing with money and facing your debt, and aversion to numbers. At the same time, I will gently take you step-by-step through the process of creating a spending plan and learning how to make it a natural part of your life.

The original program started out as a free online, audio-based curriculum. Recognizing that some people prefer to have a written guidebook, I edited the transcript of the online audio program for the print edition. Therefore, you will find the written version may not precisely match the audios.

But, I encourage you to listen to the audio program as you work through the book for a more personalized experience, kind of like listening to a friend on the phone. Just go to the website: fearlessbudgeting.wordpress.com for access to the free audio course. And, while you're there, you may want to sign up for email updates, where I'll announce additional support options and live events.

In order to keep the flow of information smooth, all links to resources mentioned in the training program are contained in the Resources handout (also at the end of this book), not in the lesson where they are mentioned.

I'm so happy that you're taking this brave first step to change your life and I look forward to helping you on this healing journey.

COURSE I
FOUNDATIONAL COURSE:

CREATING YOUR SPENDING PLAN

SECTION I:

BEFORE YOU BEGIN

• LESSON #1 •

Welcome

WELCOME TO THE FEARLESS BUDGETING Training Course for Compulsive Spenders. I'm excited to embark on this transformational journey with you. You've really exhibited great courage and willingness by embarking on this journey. I know how hard a decision it is to take steps to change your relationship with money and spending.

I feel passionate about helping people create a spending plan and learn how to use it because I know from my own experience what an essential tool it is for anyone who is serious about recovering from compulsive spending.

But before we begin, I want to talk a bit about why you haven't already done this. Many people want to create and live by a spending plan but can't even get started because just the prospect of looking at the reality of their spending or opening the envelopes from creditors or the idea of working with numbers paralyzes them. Recently, I spoke with a friend who was spinning and spiraling downward because she just can't get a grip on her spending. She said she's great with numbers, but when it comes to creating boundaries around the dollars in her own checking account, she's so freaked out about it that it all looks like Greek to her. So, if any of this describes you, this training program can help you move past those fears.

Someone recommended to another friend that she just look at her checking account daily to see where her money is going. When I heard that, I laughed, because even today, doing that without having a spending plan in place would leave me breathless and woozy. Especially today, now that I no longer compulsively spend, when I look at my checking account, I see a lot of money. Well, relatively speaking (thinking back to the days when I might have had a negative balance in my account). But still, it's a lot of money to me.

Viewing my money in that way, seeing that pile of money sitting there, would awaken the spending beast within me who would instantly come up with five different ways to spend that money IMMEDIATELY, and give me complete amnesia around the need to reserve any of those dollars for expenses.

So, no. That would not be helpful to me.

Instead, I live and breathe by the categories in my spending plan. Because my spending plan and my bank account are reconciled, which means they are accurately balanced, I can trust that the amount that is available in each category of my spending plan is really there to spend. I can't tell you the peace of mind I feel when I see my money in these individual categories rather than in one big batch. So, for instance, I know I have $645 left to spend on groceries this month, and I can also rest easy seeing that the money for my monthly bills is sitting quietly in each of their respective categories awaiting their turn to become payments.

Yes, I still have moments of desire and painful longing for something I don't have the money to buy. But I am committed to living within my means, which, for me, means living by my spending plan. I have learned that the pain of not making the purchase is not bottomless, and delayed gratification has become a cherished friend instead of an enemy.

Going from being a compulsive spender to willingly living by a spending plan is a vast undertaking. I'm not going to lie to you. It means feeling the pain of saying no to yourself. Pain, of course, being an understatement when the real feeling is that you will die if you don't give in to the yearning.

So, here's the hard truth. A spending plan won't cure you of compulsive spending. But it *is* a tool you must embrace if you are serious about recovering from compulsive spending. If you're like me, you already know this is true. Just think about how many books, courses, and spending plan software or templates you've already tried and abandoned.

Through the Fearless Budgeting training program, I'm going to walk with you through the process of creating a spending plan, and help you continue to live in clarity around your spending. Because I've been where you are, I can help you address the fear and anxiety you experience around this process in a way the financial gurus can't. And I know how to teach you the technical side of budgeting in a simple and easy way. So, I want you to feel hopeful and positive that you can accomplish this.

But, I also need to share my belief that it's imperative to include some form of recovery work around the spending addiction to succeed with any spending plan process. The part that I can't help you with, the part that no budgeting expert can teach you, is how to recover from that seemingly hopeless state of mind and body that is compulsive spending; to discover what will work for you to get you willing to say no when the demon inside of you is screaming YES; to teach you how to embrace delayed gratification instead of recoiling from it.

One thing I know for certain, trying to do this with no network of support is least likely to work. So, I urge you to find others who are walking this path with you. My path was through the Twelve Steps. But there are many avenues to recovery from compulsive spending. I do recommend that you try six Debtors Anonymous meetings. You don't have to be in debt to benefit from that program. They have phone meetings worldwide every single day as well as many in-person meetings. There is absolutely no cost to join. And you will find a network of support waiting for you with open arms.

But if that program just doesn't speak to you, try Underearners Anonymous or Recoveries Anonymous. And if the Twelve Step model just isn't your cup of tea, know that there are lots of other programs around, like SMART recovery, and even therapists specializing in compulsive spending. Just Google "Compulsive Spending Help."

But, a word of caution: if you do find a therapist, group, or program that costs money, please be very careful not to pay more than you can afford. And research it well to ensure you will find the help you need. I once heard a wonderful expression at a meeting – Do not mistake temptation for opportunity. So please keep that in mind when "shopping" for a recovery program. In my experience, if it causes you to overspend or debt, it's most likely temptation. And for me, the best network was one comprised of other compulsive spenders.

Having said all that, you can still benefit from the Fearless Budgeting Training program because you will be given the step-by-step instructions and emotional support you need to move forward to *create* your spending plan and learn how to incorporate it into your daily life. Even if you find yourself back at square one down the road, once you've gone through this process, you'll be able to pick up right where you left off with your spending plan without having to start from scratch.

And even if you aren't in recovery yet, if you feel ready to move forward with Fearless Budgeting, you may find it's just the push you need to propel you into recovery from compulsive spending.

You may ask, if I so strongly believe in the Twelve Step recovery model, why do I feel the need to provide this training program? It's because walking people through the process of creating a spending plan foundation with the level of detail and time commitment that I do is not something generally done as part of any recovery program, because people either can't commit that much time to help one person through the creation process or they're not prepared to provide the technical training down the road. But there are scores of people who need such help.

Many people in recovery have come to me after immense frustration, feeling like they're going in circles, even with all the support the program offers, because they still can't figure out how to create the foundational document needed to begin the spending plan process or, later on, they didn't understand how to use technology to track their spending when they desperately wanted to do so.

I've often spent 20 hours a week or more with one person taking them through this process or training them in using technology to track their spending plan or troubleshooting technology glitches around their spending plan. So, I've come to believe that such technical processes are outside issues that can be addressed with integrity without violating the sacred boundaries of a Twelve Step recovery program. I view the Fearless Budgeting training program as an adjunct to recovery, not a replacement.

I just want to add a note on language used in the program. I alternate using the terms living within your means, living by a spending plan, and living in recovery. Though they all mean the same thing for purposes of these lessons, what I really mean when I say "living in recovery" is a reference to healing from the addiction of compulsive spending and/or debting. In my mind, I'm referring to Twelve Step recovery, but as I've already mentioned, there are other ways to achieve that goal.

Please feel free to email me any questions, concerns, or to share your thoughts and feelings.

• LESSON #2 •

How to Take the Course and Additional Options

I JUST WANT TO TAKE a few minutes to talk to you about the ways you can proceed with the training and let you know about additional resources and support options.

How to Take the Training

The Fearless Budgeting training program is comprised of two courses:

- First is the "Foundational Course: Creating Your Spending Plan," which contains 26 lessons.
- The second course is a continuation, to be taken following the first. It's called "Working with Your Spending Plan." There are 24 lessons in that course.

The Fearless Budgeting training program is comprised of:

1. An audio for each lesson
2. A transcript for each lesson, some containing screen shots (transcripts have been edited and may, therefore, not precisely match the audio)
3. A workbook to be used with the Foundational Course: Creating Your Spending Plan (Excel or PDF)
4. A handout with resources mentioned in the training and links
5. There will be one video of my entire spending plan process (this video will be available on my YouTube channel as well as on the e-learning platform)

Though every situation is unique, generally, each course can be completed within two weeks, so you can be working with a realistic spending plan within a month!

Both courses are offered for free online. You can listen to the audio and read each lesson as you go through the course, and you'll have access to the Fearless Budgeting workbook and resources as well. I'll talk about support options in a moment.

But some people prefer to listen and/or read offline. So, you can optionally purchase:

1. A self-contained print or e-book version (e.g., Kindle) of the entire training program, which includes the workbook and resources. The book can be used without the audios to take you through the entire training.
2. A downloadable version of the complete Fearless Budgeting training program, which contains:
    - Audios for both courses in MP3 format
    - A separate copy of the Fearless Budgeting workbook in both Excel and PDF format

Support Options

If you have any questions about the training program, concepts, or instructions, you can always email me at fearlessbudgeting@gmail.com.

There is also a student discussion forum in the online training program where you can post questions and I'll reply to you there. I really encourage you to use that resource because posting in the student forum will benefit others who may have the same question that you do. Unfortunately, I had already completed the audios prior to selecting an e-learning platform. So wherever you hear me suggest that you email me with questions, comments, or suggestions, please feel free to post in the student discussion forum instead.

I'm also considering offering periodic "open office hours." This will be a time that you can call in on a conference-call line to ask me questions and get more personalized support.

So, if you haven't done so already, go ahead and sign up for the Fearless Budgeting mailing list because I'll announce the open office hours and other events through the mailing list when they become available.

Additional Resources

There are a couple of additional resources you may want to consider as you work through this training program:

- If you enjoy journaling, you may want to download the FREE PDF version of my Five-Year Recovery Journal.
- And finally, I've also written a daily reader for compulsive spenders and debtors. You may find it helpful and encouraging to read each day as you go through this process. You can check out sample pages from the "Getting Out from Going Under Daily Reader for Compulsive Debtors and Spenders" on my blog.

Please note that whenever I mention a resource, just go check out the resources handout to get the link.

We have just a few more lessons before we begin the work, but these lessons contain crucial building blocks you need before we get started.

• LESSON #3 •

So Why *Do* You Need a Spending Plan?

COMPULSIVE SPENDERS ARE GENERALLY UNDISCIPLINED. Maybe you are highly disciplined in other areas of your life, but I've yet to meet any active compulsive spender who isn't disorganized, vague, and out of control when it comes to money, and I know many compulsive spenders in recovery who still find their finances overwhelming and messy.

The reason for that has inevitably been that they still lacked clarity around their spending and debt. And I've found that people are sometimes confused about the difference between tracking their spending and living by a spending plan.

When people say they "track their numbers," it means that every time you buy something, you write down what you bought and how much you spent. It's a necessary component to figuring out the truth about your spending, but it's only the first step in a three-part process and, by itself, it won't give you the truly healing clarity you can have around your spending. For instance, if I just track my numbers, I can easily:

- Spend money that I need for rent to go to a concert because I forgot about the rent being due, and I don't get paid again in time to avoid a late fee.
- Overdraw my checking account if I don't keep track of the available balance.

It's crucial to develop a method to know before you spend money whether you can afford to buy the item. That's what a spending plan does for you. And that's the second step of the process. And by the way, in this training program, I'll be teaching you all the budgeting concepts you may find confusing, like reconciling with your bank account (in course #2), and I'll give you clear, step-by-step instructions on how to accomplish these tasks.

But what you need the support of others for is to help you get willing to live by the reality of how much money is available for what you want to purchase and to teach you how to live with the discomfort of saying no when you can't afford it. And that's the third step of the process ... without which the other two steps are unlikely to keep you from compulsively spending for long.

It's like building a house. One part of the process is gathering all the materials for your new home (tracking your numbers). Another part is putting up the walls and designing the interior (creating and living by a spending plan). Your new home could be gorgeous to look at, but without the crucial third piece – a strong foundation (recovery from the addiction) – your house will be easily destroyed.

• LESSON #4 •

Please Do Not Jump Ahead

HERE'S THE THING. IF YOU'RE embarking on this training program, it's most likely because you haven't been able to get anywhere before, and not for lack of trying. I've got a proven method to get you over the emotional hurdles to create your spending plan foundation, and to follow through for the long haul, but it just won't work if you overwhelm yourself by jumping ahead.

My training system is based on taking very, very small steps in a certain order. And I've seen it work over and over.

So, I'm asking you to trust me.

But I also implore you to not only read each lesson in order, but to do the work in a lesson (if any) before reading the next. Again, each lesson builds on the one before, and as your confidence grows, you will be able to handle the more difficult and complex parts of creating and working with a spending plan. It's just like exercising any other muscle. You need to start slowly.

I want you to succeed as so many others have. I know it's not always easy to stay motivated on your own, so please feel free to email me if you have questions or concerns.

• LESSON #5 •

Crucial Lesson Spending Plan vs. Budget

I WRESTLED WITH NAMING THIS training program for months. As you may know if you read my blog "Getting Out from Going Under" or listen to the "I Can't Stop Spending!" podcast, I despise the word budget, but I strongly believe in the act of allocating money to categories, which is the definition of budgeting. I'll go into more detail about spending plans vs. budgets in a moment. But the name "Fearless Budgeting" truly encapsulates my overriding approach ... to gently take you by the hand and help you overcome your terror around facing the truth of your spending, which is a crucial first step in the process, and to ease you into a practice that will keep you clear around your money and engaged with your spending plan ongoing. Remember, courage is not the absence of fear, but the willingness to move forward despite it.

What's the difference between a budget and a spending plan? Well, I believe a spending plan is a budget with an attitude adjustment. Budgets are tight, restrictive, punishing. Spending plans are gentle, fluid, and flexible.

That's not to say that there aren't boundaries around spending plan categories, and, therefore, pain for compulsive spenders. It's just that the way we approach a spending plan is vastly different than a budget.

Here's an example. When my life came crashing down in 2009 around my $34,000+ debt and seeing that there was no way for me to finance my son's housing and living expenses for his first year at college in the fall, I turned to a friend of mine who is not a compulsive spender for help. She had successfully wound her way out of a bleak financial situation after she'd been reckless with money. But the difference between us became apparent quickly.

"So, you're going to have to get rid of your cable TV and any other discretionary spending, and just eat canned tuna until you are out of debt," She said. "It's only for a few years." I felt the proverbial whip coming down to punish me with 1,000 lashes.

The problem for people like us (if you're a compulsive spender like me) is that we, paradoxically, spend more when we are told we can't spend at all. "Here! I'll show you!" The addict mind says to attempts to rein it in.

The financial gurus seem to think our addiction is just weakness, selfishness, and a lack of willpower. But I know that's just not true. How many times have we vowed not to binge spend or buy impulsively, only to have our deepest intentions slashed in an instant when confronted with the inability to say no to a purchase driven by that internal demon?

Most compulsive spenders feel like marionettes on a string and come to a point where the pain of what they're doing is far worse than the pain of saying no, but they feel stuck and powerless in the face of what they feel forced to do, often against their will, sometimes not thinking at all or even in a sickening variation of an alcoholic blackout.

So, I knew that my path to salvation would absolutely not involve a rigid budget wrapped in deprivation. That would just flare up an irresistible desire to escape from the pain. I knew this was true because I'd been in recovery 12 years before and paid off $22,000 of debt, though I didn't stay there after the miracle happened because I deluded myself into believing the lie that just because I was debt-free, I was no longer a compulsive spender ... so here I was, 12 years later, with $34,000+ of credit card debt, and, by the way, nothing to show for it. Still, I knew it was possible to recover again, with the debt repayment a blessed side effect.

I firmly believe that a spending plan is a required tool for a recovering compulsive spender, but it is not a cure for compulsive spending.

So, in 2009, I came back into the Twelve Step recovery program that worked for me before I stopped working it. And got the help I needed to create a balanced spending plan. And this time, I have no intention of leaving, even though I finished paying off that debt in 2016.

Last year, I heard a story on one of those financial gurus' radio shows about a guy who paid of something like $40,000 of debt in a year and a half. He did it by essentially following the guidance of my well-meaning friend - living in complete, abject deprivation until that debt was paid off. The financial guru applauded his efforts and cheered him on. To me, it sounded horrific, and a sure-fire recipe for failure. Bouncing from one extreme to the other didn't seem sane or sober. And I wondered if the gentleman was still debt-free.

Instead, I paid off my debt over the course of seven years (finishing in February of 2016), despite becoming disabled one year into my debt repayment plan and losing a chunk of my previous income. I did so while still including a small amount of discretionary spending for things like entertainment (yep, I kept the cable TV), gifts, clothes, and a vacation. That's not to say that I can buy whatever I want when I want it. Oh no. My spending plan was tight, and got substantially tighter a few years later when I lost my private disability insurance.

But while I did (and still do) have to face delaying gratification often, and sometimes must accept no as a final answer, I wasn't stripped of every spending want as some kind of punishment for the debt I had incurred. And because I paid off the debt gradually, in a balanced way that worked for me, I didn't feel the compulsion to race out and spend once the debt was finally paid off.

Of course, the recovery piece was crucial, because without that, no spending plan would have worked for me. Any limits would have felt like more than I could bear. But I can tell you with certainty that no matter how committed my recovery, a spending plan that was inflicted on me like a punishment would have likely sent me over the edge anyway.

A spending plan gives me clear and crucial boundaries around my spending. But finding the willingness not to give in to my obsession and compulsion is the gift of recovery. The spending plan shows me how much I have available to spend. Recovery teaches me how to live with delayed gratification. Together, they provide the balance that can heal the fracture of addiction, which opens the way for enhanced relationships and a much better life.

A Roadmap of Your Life

Because a spending plan is based on the reality of your life today, it's really a visual diary of you at this moment in time, almost a road map, which, if you think about it, is kind of exciting. At another point, it's going to look quite different.

For example, the spending plan of a new mother is not going to resemble that of a retired grandmother, yet it may belong to the same person at different points in her life. It can be quite a spiritual practice to look back at how your spending plan evolves over time. But it's not just that your needs change. You may find that your tracking may alternate between a high level of detail and a broader overview depending on whether you need additional clarity around certain types of spending. And that's where the flexibility of a spending plan comes in.

Where is the Flexibility in a Spending Plan?

Because a spending plan is based on conscious choices about how one spends money, once we have a strong foundation, we can modify our spending plan to meet new or changed life circumstances. And that includes having the power to temporarily or permanently modify the plan if an unexpected situation comes up.

For instance, my dog is 12 years old. I've always had a doggie insurance plan, but last month, downgraded from the premium to the basic plan because he's been so healthy. Wouldn't you know it, he suddenly needed an emergency x-ray shortly after making this change, which was not covered by the basic plan. The x-ray cost nearly $200. I only had about $20 in his medical category.

Being a compulsive spender, I know that I don't always think clearly around spending decisions, especially in an emergency situation. Because I have a network of support, I was able to talk to two people to figure out the best course of action. After discussion with each of my friends, it became clear that going back to the premium plan was actually the better option in the long run. The x-ray would be covered. And we figured out that the extra cost over the course of a year would be offset by a larger discount on services ongoing.

With the help of my friends, I moved money from other discretionary categories to ensure I would accumulate more money for non-covered services in the future. The point I'm trying to make to you is that having a spending plan made figuring out the best course of action in a highly stressful situation so much easier.

You have the same flexibility when your life circumstances change. So, if you are going back to school or having a child, or your child is graduating college, the spending plan gives you a base foundation where you can shift your spending as your priorities change. You don't have to start the process from scratch.

The beautiful part about it is that having your money in categories becomes a comfort, even when you wish there were more of it, but especially when you need to make a change on the fly, as I had to do. Panic could make me act irrationally and irresponsibly, but with a spending plan in front of me, it gives me the gift of a clear picture, so I can take a pause to consider the best choice of action.

I want to end this lesson with the reminder that the point of a spending plan is to create balance in your life between your wants and your needs. When you choose to live by a spending plan, you inevitably come face to face with your addiction when you see clearly that you can't always buy what you want when you want it. But when used in conjunction with a commitment to living within your means, a spending plan is a treasure map leading us out of the pit of destruction that our compulsive spending has dug beneath us.

OK, so the good news is that there's just one more lesson before we get down to work. And there's no bad news. So, I'm looking forward to continuing this journey with you.

• LESSON #6 •

The Foundational Document and Meeting Delayed Gratification

WE'RE GOING TO START OUT by creating your foundational document. Now, what do I mean by a "foundational document." It's *not* a spending plan. It's just a piece of paper on which you write information. That's it. Nothing scary or threatening about it. But I'd like you to think about this phase of the process as detective work where you are beginning to put together the pieces of a puzzle.

In the next lesson, when we get started, you'll understand a lot more about how this will work. But we're really going to take things very slowly, step-by-step. Eventually, the foundational document will turn into your spending plan foundation, and you'll discover your foundational number. But you don't need to know any of this yet.

So, how do you feel right now? Let's check in.

Are you feeling anxious or scared about this process? Excited? Do you want to run away? Are you annoyed because you want to know more of the details now? If you answered yes to any of these questions, consider this a practice in delayed gratification, something I will talk about at length down the road. But feel your desire to know everything right now. Feel any discomfort, tightness, or breathlessness, any frustration, irritation, or fear around this process.

Feeling these emotions won't kill you (and believe me, I used to think it would). The truth is that *facing and feeling* discomfort reduce it far more often than ignoring it or pushing it away.

So, now, please take a long, slow, deep breath in. And then, slowly release it.

And just pause in silence for a moment.

I had you do that exercise for a reason. Compulsive spenders often act impulsively when the desire hits, or when their anxiety, fear, and frustration spiral out of control. But the truth is, there is a moment, a pause, between the thought and the action. Here's an example of what I mean. You didn't stop reading to figure everything out. You didn't close the book and run away. No, you stayed, despite your feelings. And in that pause, you breathed, and sat with it.

Finding *that* pause when filled with a desperate longing to spend is the moment of Grace when you can change the situation. You can make a phone call, you can close the website page, you can get out of the store. That moment has all possibilities in it. And just recognizing that there IS a pause is huge, because, when I was compulsively spending, it seemed like the thought and the act were one and the same. In recovery, I learned how to stay in the pause without acting on my impulse until the impulse passed.

We will return to this healing breath exercise periodically throughout the training. I hope you will embrace this simple practice as a tool to turn to when the obsession and compulsion hit.

To prepare for the next lesson, please have a pencil with an eraser and either a notebook or a few pieces of printer paper. Nothing fancy. Oh, and there's no need for a calculator.

SECTION II:

BUILDING A FOUNDATION

• LESSON #7 •

Let's Begin

OK, LET'S GET STARTED. Before we begin though, I just want to reiterate that we are NOT creating a spending plan today. Nope. There's absolutely nothing to be on edge about in this exercise. We're just going to write down some information on a piece of paper. Not a spending plan.

I'm asking you to let go of any perfectionist tendencies you might have for now. Just do the exercise I'm going to give you without worrying that you aren't doing it right or you're forgetting something. It doesn't matter. It's just a warm-up exercise, but it's really important that you take the five minutes to do it.

Alright, I'm assuming you have a pencil *with* an eraser. And a piece of paper. And NO calculator. Great!

Now, we're going to start thinking about how you live your life, which is essentially, where you spend your money. We're not talking about compulsive spending. We're just making an objective list of what parts of our life our money goes to, without making any kind of judgment around it or how much we spend on any of it. It's just a list on a piece of paper. A list, you can, in fact, erase. Just words on paper. Not a spending plan.

So, just like with any brainstorming session, I want you to write down every single category of spending you can think of that is relevant to your life. Now, remember, no calculators, no numbers, and no shame or guilt. You are a detective, simply cataloging information. So, if you do have debt, just write D E B T as one among many categories. It's just a word, like frankfurter or schnitzel. No need to assign any emotion or angst to listing it. You aren't writing down *any* numbers. Just words.

For now, start to think in terms of broad categories. So, instead of writing socks, dresses, and coats, instead write clothing. Or instead of milk, bread, and paper towels, you could list Groceries and, possibly, House Supplies as a separate category. There's no way you can do this wrong. Remember, you are just starting this process. In fact, great job that you made it this far! Seriously, you could be doing something else. And certainly, it's a lot better than some things you might be doing, right?

So, I'd like you take five minutes now, right now, to make your list. No need to look at your checkbook or your bank records or search online for ideas for categories. Just write down what you think of off the top of your head. And then, I promise I'll give you plenty of category ideas.

When you've finished writing your initial list (the sloppier, the better), please go on to the next lesson. But keep this list handy. Oh, and, again, please spend no more than five minutes doing this exercise.

• LESSON #8 •

Handouts for Building Your Foundation

I HOPE THE EXERCISE IN Lesson #7 was easy and simple for you ... and maybe even just a little bit fun? Or maybe not. Before we move on, let's just take that pause for a moment to breath in slowly and deeply.

And then breathe out slowly as well.

And sit for a moment in that pause.

In order to work through this part of the course, you will need worksheets. Since you have the print version of the book, you will find the worksheets in the first lesson associated with it. There is also a printable PDF version of the workbook, which you can download. And for those who prefer to work in a spreadsheet, I've created an Excel workbook with the six different worksheets in it and a page of instructions.

For those who prefer to work in a spreadsheet, I've created an Excel workbook with six different worksheets in it and a page of instructions. For those who like to work with pencil and paper, I've created a printable PDF version of the workbook. This lesson contains the downloadable zipped file.

Please do not jump ahead. It is important that we work through this workbook one step at a time. Slow and steady.

In the spreadsheet version of the workbook, I've automated all the calculations to make it super simple. To ensure you don't accidentally overwrite the automation, I've protected everything in the workbook except the areas in which you'll enter information. Those sections are in light pink. I'll explain in more detail as we work on each worksheet.

If you are using the PDF version, then you *will* need a calculator down the road, but don't worry, you'll be ready for it when the times comes. The PDF version contains page numbers for each worksheet. You're going to want to keep this handy, so you can easily find the worksheet referenced in each lesson.

Please bear in mind that this workbook may not cover every single person's situation. But using them for this course will give you all the skills you need to adapt the worksheets to your own life situation. For now, when you come across anything in the workbook that doesn't apply to you, just skip it.

You'll find links to all the resources I mention in the Resources section at the end of this book and in the PDF Resources handout.

• LESSON #9 •

Categories

ALRIGHT. WE'RE NOW READY TO BEGIN using our workbook. If you've downloaded the PDF or Excel version, go ahead and open it. And please take out the list you made in lesson #7.

When you have the workbook in front of you, please go to worksheet #1 (also located at the end of this lesson). In it, you'll see a list of categories. These are the categories that I think most people need in their personal spending plan. I call them master categories because they may contain a lot of different types of spending as subcategories.

Now take a moment and look to see if any of your categories aren't on my list. If so, you'll be able to add them easily. But hold off on that for a moment. And also note if there are categories that you may not have thought about, but you may find useful.

I'm going to go into detail about subcategories, or what types of spending might be included in master categories, in the next lesson. But for now, let's just briefly talk about two items on this list.

1. Taxes - This is for personal taxes. I'm going to talk further about taxes and tracking expenses for small businesses and hobbies in lesson #14.
2. Debt Repayment. We're not even going to think about that for now. We'll get to it ... later.

Remember, we're still just making a list. I know some of you will feel anxious or even panicked and upset because you don't have money for some of these discretionary categories I listed. Again, this is not a spending plan, and one thing we're doing here is including all categories that make for a balanced life.

Surely, even if you can't afford entertainment or a vacation today, you'd like to be able to afford those things some time, right? So, why not have it in the list? I'm not very oooogy goooogy new age-y, but I do think it can't hurt to include aspirational categories, because I believe a spending plan is about balance. And maybe not today, but some day, you will be able to fund these categories if you stay committed to living by your spending plan and within your means.

I can feel some of you becoming increasingly anxious, as would be normal for anyone going through this process. But again, I reiterate my mantra that what we are doing right now is not creating a spending plan, just a list. It's words on paper. And it's OK for you to relax and not infuse this list with any negative connotations, shame, or judgment.

So, I'd like to stop here for a moment to take a breath and pause, as we've done before. Take a long, slow deep breath in. Release it slowly. And pause.

Now, it is possible that there is a master category I have missed. So, I have included ten blank areas where you can include categories from your earlier brainstorming session that may not be listed. However, you may find that those categories may actually fit as a subcategory for one that I've already listed. So, go ahead and add it for now, but know that you can always delete, or erase, it later.

If you're using the spreadsheet, just remember that you will come back to sheet #1 to add, edit, or delete your master categories. They will automatically update throughout the workbook when you edit them in worksheet #1.

Please don't skip any lessons now that you have the workbook. It's important that I explain it to you, so you don't get overwhelmed. We're going to brainstorm together, and you may find you think of additional master categories later. Remember, I told you that one of the keys to succeeding with this process is to take things really slow, especially as we move further into it.

As always, feel free to email me with any concerns or questions or just to let me know how you're feeling.

Worksheet #1 MASTER CATEGORIES

Universal categories most people need.

- Housing
- Utilities
- Insurance
- Transportation
- Grocery (includes personal care)
- Persona Business
- Medical
- Wardrobe
- Gifts
- Charity
- Entertainment
- Vacations
- Technology
- Savings
- Taxes
- Debt Repayment

Special Circumstances

- Pet
- Childcare
- College
- Partner

Add other master categories below

END OF MASTER CATEGORIES WORKSHEET

• LESSON #10 •

Master and Subcategories

IN THE LAST LESSON, WE went over a list of master categories that most people need. And then, you added any categories you had come up with that aren't in the list. Master categories are broad containers. They generally contain subcategories, or like items, grouped together. For instance, doctor, dentist, and prescriptions could be subcategories of the medical master category.

We're now going to look at worksheet #2, which contains a list of all the master categories from sheet #1. Plus, I've filled in some suggestions for subcategories. You'll find a copy of this worksheet at the end of this lesson. If you're using the Excel spreadsheet, all the categories are automatically copied into worksheet #2.

Note: If you find there isn't enough room for all your subcategories, you can add additional master categories. For instance, let's say you have more housing subcategories than there are available lines. All you need to do is create a new master category called "Housing#2" in which you list your additional housing subcategories. Remember, this foundation will eventually be transferred to whatever method you're going to use to actually work with your spending plan, so you'll be able to merge them into one master category later.

Again, remember that we're still just making a list and now, we're going to dig a little bit deeper to think more in-depth. Remember, if, at any time, this process feels overwhelming, just take a break. There's no rush to get this done. I know you'd like to have it together, but if you push yourself further than you can handle in one session, you're going to walk away without getting through to the other side and experiencing the benefits of Fearless Budgeting. And I promise you that the other side will be well worth waiting for.

So, remember to take it easy and take it slow. This is a long lesson, so I suggest you work along with it. Pause the lesson after I talk about a few categories and think about additional subcategories you might add, delete any you don't need, or move a subcategory to another master category. If you're working on paper, just scratch through subcategories I've suggested and write them in where you feel they better fit if you need them. On the computer, just delete any that I've written in and type them in where you'd prefer if you need them.

Getting Specific and Grouping Similar Types of Spending

Now, I've given you lots of ideas for subcategories, but again, it's important to keep in mind that this document is yours, so you may end up grouping things in a whole different way. And that's fine. But to get started, I think it's helpful for you to see one way to group items. I'm going to walk through some other options a bit later.

Right now, you're just getting crystal clear about what types of spending comprise your reality. You may not track to this level of detail once you have a spending plan. But it's crucial to lay it all out in this foundational document so you make a decision with as much clarity as possible about the level of detail you need when you do turn it into a spending plan down the road. And I urge you to err on the side of more detail in the beginning to get the maximum benefit from this process. It's still beneficial to me to have lots of subcategories. And takes no more time to maintain because I'm now so used to tracking my money this way.

Believe me, I've had my experiences trying to group things in broad categories. That works great if you have difficulty *spending* money. But for a compulsive spender, I think it's a dangerous path. Once I get vague, I get confused, and then I get overwhelmed trying to figure it out, and then I give up. So, I implore you to keep going with this process and just dump *all* your ideas for subcategories on the paper for now.

Personal Income Tax Deductions

I want to first talk to you about how I group items that are eligible for a personal income tax deduction. While tax laws are changing, up until now, for instance, you've been able to deduct charitable giving and medical expenses. What I do is put a prefix in front of items that are tax deductible, so when I need to gather and total the information during tax time, it's really easy using my budgeting software.

For instance, in worksheet #2, look at the third Master Category - Insurance. You'll see Health Insurance listed third as a subcategory. But, you'll also see the letters "TD" in front of the word Health. I add the letters "TD" (for tax deductible) in front of any items that I can deduct on my federal income tax. If you have a small business or money-making hobby, in a later lesson I'm going to walk you through how to name and group your business spending plan categories and subcategories to make reporting simple, whether you do your own taxes or have an accountant do them.

If this still seems confusing, please send me an email and I'll further clarify.

Thoughts on Master and Subcategories

So, now, let's go through these master and subcategories. I'm not going to go over every single subcategory because you can see the list for yourself, but I do want to give you my thoughts on each master category.

Housing

Now, here's an example of my making a choice in how I group items. I put house insurance under a master category called Insurance. However, you might eliminate the Insurance category altogether and prefer to put insurance subcategories into their relevant master category. So, car insurance could go under Transportation, health insurance under Medical, and house, or renter's, insurance under Housing. There are no category police and no right way to do this. I'm giving you this outline, but I want to encourage you to make the list your own and group items as makes sense to you. Other categories that might go under Housing would be paying for pest control or appliance service contracts.

Utilities

You may have other utilities that I haven't listed. Or your cable bill may already include the cell phone, Internet, and TV service on one bill. In that case, you may want to simply make one subcategory called Cable Bill and delete the Internet and TV subcategories.

Insurance

As I said earlier, you might group all insurance subcategories under this master category or put each one in a related master category instead. And don't forget, if a category doesn't apply to you, just skip or delete it.

Transportation

This doesn't just include a vehicle, but can include public transportation, transit or toll road pass, gas, etc. You might want to put a category for new car to give you a place to start accumulating funds. (And, remember, you could instead, put a new car category under the Savings master category.) This would also be a good place to list vehicle repairs.

Grocery

I grouped together a number of broad sub-categories. Of course, you can't account for every single item. Sometimes, something will come up that you aren't sure where it goes. So, you'll decide at the time. For instance, let's say you bought a can opener. That could be a House Supply in this Grocery master category or it could go into the Housing master category under Small Appliances.

Personal care as a subcategory within the Grocery master category can be as broad as you want it to be while still giving you clarity. Here's an example. Because I so rarely buy makeup, I would just take money for that out of this subcategory. But someone else who buys a lot of makeup may want to assign an entire master category to skin care/makeup. Or, you may want to create a Personal Care master category.

You'll note that I included a category for coffee out. For many people, it's crucial to track this category separately, at least initially, if you buy coffee out frequently. I will tell you that it's one area that shocks people when they learn how much they spend on coffee out. But that's not your concern right now.

Personal Business

Again, you may have other types of items to add here, but I wanted to give you my list of items that would fit.

Medical

Now we come to the Medical category. So, first, you'll see a few medical subcategories that have "TD" in front of them. These would be items that you can deduct on your personal tax return. With changes to the tax code, I'm not sure whether this will still be true, but now you understand the concept ... and it may be relevant to other categories. Also, travel to and from the doctor is currently deductible, so you might want to think about tracking your mileage if you have significant medical bills and travel to and from doctors, dentists, etc.

I've put a link in the Resources handout to the IRS publication (PDF) that lists all eligible medical items you can deduct. Beginning on page 5, there is a very simple, easy to read list of items by category that you can deduct. It's not convoluted and complex like most things tax-related. I've also put a link to the user-friendly TurboTax checklist of deductible medical items. Unfortunately, there are plenty of items that you *can't* include as part of your medical deduction.

The rest of the medical items in the workbook list do not have the "TD" prefix because they are not tax-deductible. This would include supplements, medical books on conditions you might have, non-traditional or alternative health care providers who don't take insurance. For instance, I have a health coach who has been a great help to me, but no way I can deduct his fee. However, it's worth asking if they work with a covered medical provider. You never know. If you aren't tracking personal tax deductions, just remove the letters "TD" from the subcategories.

Wardrobe

You can see I split this master category into four subcategories: accessories, clothing, shoes, and makeup. Now, as I said earlier, I don't need a subcategory for makeup as I buy it so rarely. Or you may feel that makeup belongs elsewhere, maybe in the Personal Care subcategory in Grocery or in a master category of its own.

I want you to feel free to mold this list to fit your life. Since we're talking about wardrobe, I'll say that you can make this foundational document fit you like a glove or the perfect shoe for your foot! 😊 Speaking of that, maybe you think shoes belong in accessories, for instance, or, again, in its own master category.

Gifts

My experience is that subdividing this master category is the best way to approach gifts if you are a compulsive spender. For now, just keep in mind that you aren't dealing with numbers, and you don't have to make any decisions about how much to put into any category. As you can see, I've come up with Holiday, Birthday, Illness, Work, and Other Celebrations, such as weddings or anniversaries. You may not need all these subcategories or you may have others I haven't thought about.

Instead of making one subcategory called birthdays, I actually have a separate subcategory for each person for whom I buy a birthday gift. It makes it much easier to track how much I spend on each person.

You could do the same thing with holiday gifts. Especially with the Gifts category, where my guilt and ego often drive me to spend more than I can afford, more clarity is better for me. So, I urge you to follow my suggestions here. For example:

Birthday Gifts
Spouse
Son
Daughter-in-Law
Niece #1
Niece #2
Nephew #1

Charity

I've divided this into four subcategories:

1. 7th tradition for those who are in recovery programs
2. Any specific charitable organizations you contribute to regularly
3. Tithing for those who engage in this practice
4. And other charity, which could cover small amounts given at the grocery store register, to school groups, in passing, or during the holidays.

I have my own opinion about tithing (see Resources for a link to my podcast episode on this topic), but I will simply say that while I strongly believe in charitable giving, I don't believe in debting to do so. And I believe that there are many deeply meaningful ways to give that don't involve money, and which may provide even greater benefit to the recipient. Just delete the charity subcategories that don't apply to your situation and add any additional that do.

Entertainment

Again, as with wardrobe and grocery, this can be as broad or specific as you need it to be for clarity around your spending. I made subcategories for Books, Movies, Hobbies, Theater, and an Other subcategory, for something that might come up that I haven't thought about. For instance, that might be an art or some other type of class, or maybe I decide to start going to Toastmasters to learn how to be more comfortable with public speaking.

If your finances are so tight right now that you don't see how you'll ever be able to afford anything, take a pause here. Remember, this is just a list, a list of categories that make up a balanced life. If you were already living in balance around your spending today, you wouldn't need this training program, right?

So, I'm going to ask you to include an Entertainment master category and at least two subcategories for things you would like, plus a subcategory called Other Entertainment to get you started.

Vacation

This was a hard one for me. I never took vacations. But having now done so solvently, I can tell you that it's important to list it, even if it seems far, far away from your present reality. If you are someone who is able to take vacations, then why not set up a few subcategories, like flights, hotels, tips, food, transportation, and a subcategory for unexpected travel expenses, because I've found it inevitable that something comes up that you haven't thought about.

Technology

This includes repair and replacement. I never thought about this, and every time something broke, I was in a panic trying to figure out how to buy a replacement. Again, making this list is a completely separate issue from assigning a dollar amount to any category yet. It's just a reality that eventually, your computer, monitor, tablet, printer, cell phone, Kindle, etc., will need replacement. And I know I have to buy printer cartridges and new USB cables every couple of months, so technology accessories are important as well.

Savings

OK, I can hear you telling me that you don't have any money available to save. I understand. It doesn't matter because, again, this is just a list. And a balanced spending plan ideally has some type of savings.

I, personally, have always had a hard time with the concept of savings. Money literally burned a hole in my pocket, and my spending addiction drove me to spend it as fast as it came in. Actually, faster, which is why I've ended up with six figures of debt over my adult life that I've paid off in various chunks, the last being that $34,000, which I finished paying off in 2016. But, through recovery, I am now able to tolerate having money accumulate in my categories and sit in my bank account. It's a miracle, indeed.

Emergency Savings

First, emergencies. That would be a category for small emergencies. So, for instance, you may have a vehicle repair category, which you will (yes, you will) allow to accrue over time. But let's say you get a flat tire, and you don't have enough in your Vehicle Repair category today. Or your hot water heater breaks, and you don't have enough to cover it from your Home Repairs category.

This subcategory is for spending in the hundreds to complement other categories where money builds up. Generally, you wouldn't keep more than $1,000 in an emergency fund. And I know that today, that may sound like all the money in the world to you. And that's alright. Again, we're working toward building a balanced financial life. And knowledge is power around what that means.

Retirement Savings

Next is retirement. Some of you may have a 401K through work. If you are putting some money away there, you don't necessarily need to include a retirement category in your personal spending plan because it's already been deducted from your paycheck.

For everyone else, it's important that such a category exists. Whether you are close to retirement age or you're just starting out in life, it's important to just list it as part of the reality of balanced living.

Income Replacement

And finally, there is income replacement. That would ideally contain six months of income in case you lose your job or are otherwise unable to work.

To Sum Up on Savings Subcategories

So, those are the three essential savings subcategories. You may want to add savings subcategories for other goals in life. This exercise is the perfect opportunity for you to list everything that you dream of doing in the future. Please don't associate this exercise with lack of money. We're just capturing a snapshot of your life.

This could be a great opportunity for you to see your dreams spelled out on paper. If you want to go back to school or start a business, just write it down. Or maybe you want to jump out of a plane, learn to scuba dive, travel to India, or take a safari. Whatever you yearn to do or have, even if it feels completely out of reach, this is where you want to write it down. It's not hurting anything to be on this list. And it's got to feel good to get it on paper and see it clearly spelled out.

Taxes

You may use this category to hold back a percentage of taxable interest or other earnings that don't automatically get taken out of your paycheck. I also included this here for anyone who might have a hobby or craft where they occasionally sell items. Maybe you're trying to make a business out of your hobby and you're just starting out. Or you're a freelancer who doesn't have taxes taken out of your check. I know too many people who spent all the money they earn from such income and had a big problem when it came time to pay taxes. I'll talk more about taxes in the lesson on Small Business and Hobby Tax Reporting Made Easy.

Coming Up: Special Circumstances

So, that's it for the spending categories most people have - other than debt, which I'll discuss in a separate lesson. If you feel overwhelmed, then just take a break. There's no rush in getting this done.

We'll be getting to special circumstances, like pets, relationships, children, weddings, and more in the next lesson.

WORKSHEET #2 MASTER AND SUBCATEGORIES WITH AMOUNTS

TIPS & EXPLANATION

I group related categories together (subcategories) under one heading (master category). I find it makes it easier for me to manage when similar items are grouped together. For instance, dentist, doctor, and prescription could all be subcategories under the Medical master category.

Note on tax deductible items: I use a prefix on all subcategories that are tax deductible for personal taxes, such as certain medical expenses. The prefix I use is "TD" so, for instance, I would create a TDPrescription category, since prescriptions are tax deductible (for now, anyway).

These are subcategory suggestions. But it's your spending plan, so change, add, or remove whatever doesn't work for you. You can group items together differently – for instance, you may want to put makeup under grocery or put homeowner's insurance under housing.

No Miscellaneous category! Every penny should be allocated to an actual named category. If you truly aren't sure where an item should go, then, create a Temporary Savings category and don't spend out of it. Move the money into other specific categories once you know what they will be.

END OF TIPS & EXPLANATION

Skip categories not relevant to you.

MASTER Category	SUBCATEGORY	Monthly Payment	Notes and Tips (If paid weekly, divide by 4 and put total here. See Lesson #22)
Housing	Rent/Mortgage		
	Small Appliances		
	Large Appliances		
	Decorating		
Master Category Total	Repair		
	Warranties		
	Appliance Service Contracts		
	Pest Control		
	Property Tax - due April		
Utilities	Electric		
	Gas		
	Water		
	Cable		
Master Category Total	Internet		
	Cell Phone		

Skip categories not relevant to you.

MASTER Category	SUBCATEGORY	Monthly Payment	Notes and Tips (If paid weekly, divide by 4 and put total here. See Lesson #22)
Insurance	Car		
	House/apartment		
	TDHealth insurance		
Master Category Total			
Transportation	Car payment		
	Gas		
	Repair		
Master Category Total			

Skip categories not relevant to you.

MASTER Category	SUBCATEGORY	Monthly Payment	Notes and Tips (If paid weekly, divide by 4 and put total here. See Lesson #22)
Grocery	Food		Paper towels, dish liquid, etc.
	House Supplies		
	Restaurant		
	Personal Care		Q-tips, cotton balls, hair care, etc.
	Coffee out		
Master Category Total			
Personal Business	Postage		Paper and toner, etc.
	Printer supplies		Envelopes and pens, etc.
	Stationery		Checks, ATM or annual credit card fees, etc.
	Bank and Credit Card Fees		
Master Category Total			

Skip categories not relevant to you.

MASTER Category	SUBCATEGORY	Monthly Payment	Notes and Tips (If paid weekly, divide by 4 and put total here. See Lesson #22)
Medical	TDDoctor		You may also be able to claim mileage to and from doctors on your taxes. See Resources handout for a link to a TurboTax help page on deductible medical expenses.
	TDDentist		
	TDPrescriptions		
	TDMedical Appliances		
	Supplements		
	Books on conditions		
Master Category Total			
Wardrobe	Accessories		Purse, hair clips, hats, etc.
	Clothing		
	Shoes		
	Makeup		
Master Category Total			

FEARLESS BUDGETING

Skip categories not relevant to you.

MASTER Category	SUBCATEGORY	Monthly Payment	Notes and Tips (If paid weekly, divide by 4 and put total here. See Lesson #22)
Gifts	Holiday		
	Birthday		
	Illness		
	Work		Weddings and anniversaries, etc.
	Other celebrations		You may want to make a subcategory for specific people's birthday or holiday gifts in the pink area.
Master Category Total			

• 49 •

Skip categories not relevant to you.			Notes and Tips (If paid weekly, divide by 4 and put total here. – see Lesson #22)
MASTER Category	SUBCATEGORY	Monthly Payment	
Charity	7th Tradition		For Twelve Step donations to meetings
	Specific charity		
	Tithing		
	Other charity		
Master Category Total			
Entertainment	Books		
	Movies		
	Hobby		You can also name each type of hobby separately, such as "sewing" or "knitting."
	Theater		
	Other		
Master Category Total			

FEARLESS BUDGETING

Skip categories not relevant to you.

MASTER Category	SUBCATEGORY	Monthly Payment	Notes and Tips (If paid weekly, divide by 4 and put total here. - see Lesson #22)
Vacations	Vacation Bucket		
	Flights		
	Car		
	Food		
	Entertainment		
	Tips		
	Buffer		
Master Category Total			
Technology	Computer		
	Tablet		
	Phone		
	Accessories		
Master Category Total			

Skip categories not relevant to you.

MASTER Category	SUBCATEGORY	Monthly Payment	Notes and Tips (If paid weekly, divide by 4 and put total here. - see Lesson #22)
Savings	Emergency fund		Suggested-no more than $1,000 to offset emergency costs that you may not have sufficient funds to cover.
	Retirement		
	Income Replacement		Six months of salary in case you are out of work.
Master Category Total			
Taxes	Federal Income tax		
	State tax		
Master Category Total			

FEARLESS BUDGETING

Skip categories not relevant to you.			Notes and Tips
MASTER Category	SUBCATEGORY	Monthly Payment	(If paid weekly, divide by 4 and put total here. – see Lesson #22)
Debt Repayment	Copy information from Worksheet #3		Write the amount from Worksheet #3, Total Monthly Payments, under Master Category Total
Master Category Total			

• 53 •

Your Additional Master & Subcategories

MASTER Category	SUBCATEGORY	Monthly Payment	Notes and Tips (If paid weekly, divide by 4 and put total here. See Lesson #22)
Master Category Total			
Master Category Total			
Master Category Total			

Skip categories not relevant to you.

Your Additional Master & Subcategories

Skip categories not relevant to you.

MASTER Category	SUBCATEGORY	Monthly Payment	Notes and Tips (If paid weekly, divide by 4 and put total here. See Lesson #22)
	Master Category Total		
	Master Category Total		
	Master Category Total		
	Master Category Total		

Skip categories not relevant to you.

MASTER Category	SUBCATEGORY	Monthly Payment	Notes and Tips (If paid weekly, divide by 4 and put total here. See Lesson #22)
Master Category Total			
Master Category Total			
Master Category Total			

• L E S S O N   # 1 1 •

Special Circumstances

I WANT TO TALK BRIEFLY about a few special categories that may not apply to everyone. As always, if you think of any I left out, please let me know. I'm also going to talk about planning a wedding and give a few tips to Debtors Anonymous members. If you are using the spreadsheet, you'll find special circumstances begin on line #186 of sheet #2. If you're using the PDF version, they start on page 13. In the print or e-book version, they are at the end of this lesson

I'm not going to read the list for each of these situations as you have it in the workbook. I'm just going to go over certain items.

Pets

Our pets are as beloved as children to us. And, like children, there are costs associated with raising them. Some are essential, like food and medical. My dog is now 12 years old. As far as toys and treats, it took me a lot of years of buying toys to learn that he loves just a few and I didn't need to keep buying him new ones. That was hard because I love buying presents. It also helped that his digestion became too sensitive for treats and bones. Once a year or so, I'll get him a new nylon bone to chew on, and he still has the thousand other toys from the years before lying around.

You could easily miss seeing how much you're spending on pet toys and treats. If you have a pet, I urge you to track these subcategories. And I strongly suggest, at least in the beginning, that you separate treats from your pets' Food subcategory.

Childcare

Next is the category of Childcare. I created a lot of subcategories to help you gain clarity around your costs. Again, combine, eliminate, or add subcategories as you see fit. If you have children, it's never too early to consider saving toward college or trade school for them.

I wish I had begun doing this when my son was an infant, putting $5 or even $1 a month into such a category as an aspiration. But it all seemed so far away, yet it arrived in the blink of an eye. You can read more about how preparing for my son to go to college caused me to hit my financial bottom in 2009 in an article I wrote for The Billfold (see the Resources handout for link).

Marriage or Partnership

If you are in a relationship and you are "in charge" of all, or part of, the household spending, here are some suggestions to address special issues. But, please note that I'm going to go into more detail about this in Course #2: "Working with Your Spending Plan." I'm going to use the word partner for simplicity's sake here, but know that this includes spouse, husband, wife, significant other, or the person in your life with whom you share expenses.

There are many ways that partners divide up tracking spending. I don't want to over-complicate this topic, so let me just give you a couple of suggestions:

- If you are only responsible for certain categories of spending in the household, then *your* spending plan only needs to reflect those categories. For instance, I know someone who receives a monthly allowance from her partner and is responsible for grocery and childcare expenses as well as her own personal care. Therefore, she wouldn't include utilities and home repairs, for instance, in her spending plan.
- You may be the one who gives the monthly allowance to your partner. In that case, your spending plan would include all categories, other than the ones for which your partner is responsible. But *you'd* have one master or subcategory for your partner, which might be called "Allowance" (or even just their name).
- It's a bit more complicated when partners combine their income and spend out of joint accounts. You will include all master and subcategories for both of you in the spending plan. What I would advise is that *you* take on the responsibility of keeping track of the spending, since you are the one training for it. Please don't worry. By the time you finish this training, you will be well-prepared to do so.

Just as with childcare, including partner spending in your spending plan is just a matter of including the necessary master and subcategories.

How to manage a spending plan with a partner can be complicated. For instance, what do you do if you are living by a spending plan, but your partner refuses to do so and overspends? How do you navigate this new way of relating to money when someone else is involved? For the moment, we'll table this topic. But I promise I'll talk a lot more about it later on in Course #2.

If you think your partner is open to the idea of living by a spending plan, and supportive of your efforts to develop one, you might show them your categories and ask for input. There may be categories you haven't thought about. The sooner you get partner buy-in, the easier it will be when it's time to actually make decisions based on the spending plan.

But please don't do this if you don't feel ready to include your partner in these efforts. Remember, we're just creating the foundation right now. You can always add in categories later. There will be plenty of time and opportunity to include your partner in the process down the road.

Again, I'll go into more detail about navigating a relationship once you're actually working with a spending plan, in Course #2. I know you probably have a lot of questions on this topic, so just keep track of your questions, and if they aren't answered in the later relationship lesson, please email me and I'll answer them.

Planning a Wedding

Recently, a student asked me about how to begin creating a wedding spending plan. It's the same process you use with any other type of spending. First, you'll write down master categories and then subcategories. But her question piqued my interest and I did a search on spending plan categories for a wedding.

I was excited to find just what you'll need on a website called APracticalWedding.com. I've put the link in this lesson, and in the resources handout, to a perfect post on that website by Alyssa Griffith called "How to Create a Perfect (For You) Wedding Budget." But the coolest part is that she also created a spreadsheet with all the master and subcategories you'd need, along with the percentage of your total budget you'd generally have to spend in each. You'll also find the link to that fantastic spreadsheet in the resources handout.

For Debtors Anonymous Members

If you're a member of the Debtors Anonymous Twelve Step program, you will most likely engage in Pressure Relief Groups (or PRG's). That is where two other recovering compulsive debtors work with a third on spending issues. For instance, they will help you refine your spending plan, come up with emergency or short-term plans for unexpected circumstances, trips, etc., and share their experience, strength, and hope around windfalls and big-ticket items you may want to purchase.

If you are in this fellowship, I strongly suggest you add a Savings subcategory called "PRG To Be Allocated." For some DA members, any money received, other than paychecks, over a certain amount (like $100), goes into such a subcategory, and a decision about how to allocate such money is done in conjunction with a PRG team.

So, that's all I wanted to add about special situations. I'll see you in the next lesson.

FEARLESS BUDGETING

MASTER Category	SUBCATEGORY	Monthly Payment	Notes and Tips (If paid weekly, divide by 4 and put total here. - see Lesson #22)
		Skip categories not relevant to you.	
		Special Circumstances	
Pet	Food		
	Medical		Procedures, shots, flea and tick, office visits.
	Pet insurance		
	Toys		Track to be sure spending is balanced - you can combine Toys with Treats.
Master Category Total	Treats		
	Pet-sitting		
	Equipment		Tags, leashes, and harnesses, etc.
	Training		
	Licenses		Rabies tag and annual pet license, etc.
	Supplements		
Childcare	School fees		Private/religious school tuition, home schooling fees, etc.
	School supplies		
	School events and fundraisers		
	Outside interest classes		
	Camp		
	Toys/hobbies		
	Books		
	Allowance		
	Entertainment		
	Clothing		
Childcare continued on next page...	Daycare		
	Medical		

Skip categories not relevant to you.			Notes and Tips
MASTER Category	SUBCATEGORY	Monthly Payment	(If paid weekly, divide by 4 and put total here. - see Lesson #22)
CHILDCARE CONTINUED FROM PREVIOUS PAGE			
	College Savings		
Master Category Total			
College	Tuition		
	Fees		
	Housing		
	Living expenses		
	Allowance		
	Medical		
	Travel		
Master Category Total			

Skip categories not relevant to you.		Monthly Payment	Notes and Tips (If paid weekly, divide by 4 and put total here. - see Lesson #22)
MASTER Category	SUBCATEGORY		
Partner	Allowance		If you just give a lump sum monthly, you may just keep it simple and not include specific subcategories here. Or, if you are responsible for all the spending, you might want to include additional subcategories.
Master Category Total			

• LESSON #12 •

Is There a Miscellaneous Category?

I WANT YOU TO NOTICE that there is no Miscellaneous category. That's because you're going to learn to assign every penny to a specific category. This is a crucial concept. While money may need to be moved *between* categories, one of the keys to making a spending plan work for a compulsive spender is not having money just floating out there with no intention around its use. That attitude empowers vagueness, which is deadly to a compulsive spender.

The more precisely you can assign your money, the easier it will be on you to resist impulse spending because you'll learn how to look at your categories, individually and respectfully, to determine whether you can buy something.

Of course, doing this is not a magic bullet, but it's one big step you can take to help keep you from compulsive spending. It's like creating a moat around your house. While it's still possible for you to cross when the bridge is up, it's a barrier that might make you think twice.

Now, remember, this document is not set in stone. You are going to massage it and buff it and alter it until it fits you like a glove. This is just your first pass at brain dumping all the ways your money is spent. It's not a judgment; it's a list. This document is going to become a visual diary of you at this moment in time. So, there's no pressure to try to make it perfect out of the gate.

Earlier, I spoke about having more or less detail as you need it. Here's an example from my own life. Let's take the Groceries master category. You'll notice that I separated food from house supplies. There have been times that I combined the two into one subcategory called Grocery Store because I didn't think I needed the additional clarity. But when I kept running out of food money way before the end of the month, I realized I needed to start tracking how much I was spending on house supplies. So, I made it a separate sub-category with its own money allocated to it and everything fell into place.

In the next lesson, I'm going to talk about the debt category. If you don't have debt, congratulations! You can move on to the lesson on "Small Business and Hobby Tax Reporting" or on to the "Next Step" lesson if you don't have a small business or money-making hobby.

But if you do have debt, please be sure to listen to this lesson. I talk from my own experience, coming from accumulating and paying off tens of thousands of dollars of debt over the course of my adult life. I know the anxiety that even the mention of your debts can evoke. But this is where it's important to face your fears around the topic. And your first step is to listen to the next lesson.

• LESSON #13 •

About Your Debts

DEBT. THAT DREADED CATEGORY. Before we start talking about this category, I think it's time for us to pause and...

Take a long, slow, deep breath in.

Breathe out...

And pause.

In this lesson, we're not going to address the issue of future debt, so you can relax. This lesson is just about the debt that you already have. It's more to just help you move forward with creating your foundational document. And not, in any way, a statement or a judgment about the past.

I understand that your anxiety and probably your blood pressure just shot up at the very mention of the word "debt." If you are in debt, you know that you must somehow find the courage to face the truth of it. Again, courage is not being fearless. It's doing the hard part despite being scared witless. Despite wanting to run away.

Here's where you get to see that you won't die, you won't faint, and you won't fall into a bottomless pit of spiders, snakes, bears, or whatever most terrifies you, by looking it squarely in the face and writing it down. I know from my own experience that these dreadful feelings will pass if you face them.

What you are doing takes tremendous courage. It does. And you will see, I promise you, that if you face down your demons, they will fold when they see they can't deter you. They may make you feel awful for a while, they may try to scare you, panic you, and make you doubt this process that you're engaged in.

But they're paper tigers. I know they are because I was once where you were. And now, I'm debt-free, and I have lived within my means since 2009. And this is despite becoming disabled in 2010 and losing half my salary a few years later. Being in debt, whether $500 or $500,000 doesn't change the fact that *you are a not your debt.* You have a right to live a balanced life. Please say that out loud. *I am not my debt. And I have a right to live a balanced life.*

I am not my debt. And I have a right to live a balanced life.

There is no debtors' prison. The prison of pain in which you find yourself is due to your compulsive spending demons driving you to satisfy an insatiable appetite, and your fear that they will beat you to a bloody pulp if you even attempt to stop doing so. They intimidate you by making you feel like you will die, literally die, if you don't buy the next compulsive or impulsive item ... over and over again. And they make you feel small and ashamed after you binge.

But I promise you, and I know this for a fact, that those demonic forces will lose strength as yours increases by not giving in to those voices, those feelings, that compulsion, those lies, though I know this seems impossible to believe today.

Take a close look at what has happened to you around facing your debts. Maybe you have chosen to live in complete vagueness, and you don't even know how much you owe or to whom you owe it.

Maybe you have stacks of creditor letters sitting in a pile in the corner of your house. Or maybe you have thrown away every one of those letters.

Maybe you don't answer your phone because you're terrified it's a creditor. So, you live day after day in this hellish existence where it seems like putting your fingers in your ears and singing lalalalalala will make it all just disappear. But still, it tears you up inside.

I not only understand, I empathize, because I was there. But what we are going to do, slowly, very slowly, is discover that looking at the truth around your debt is not going to reveal a monster you imagine is going to rip you limb from limb or a debt collector who will find his way into your home and drag you off to debtors' prison. But for today, remember that, in this moment, all is OK. You are listening to this lesson and taking a huge leap to improve your situation.

Your addict mind doesn't want you to believe that you can survive knowing the truth about your debt. But I'm telling you, walking into the sunlight of truth is the most healing balm there is. Information and clarity around your debt can give you the courage that living in the anxiety of terminal vagueness destroys.

Again, let this be your mantra: *I am NOT my debt. I have a right to live a balanced life.*

You do not have to punish yourself because of your debt. And your creditors are not your master.

What you do have to do is find the right weapons to win each battle against these internal demons until you've won the war. This exercise is a step in doing just that. The fact that you are engaged in this process and are willing to face the truth around your spending and, yes, your debt, tells your addiction that **you mean business**.

Your addiction is going to find all kinds of clever, sly, devious ways to distract you, to draw you away, to doubt the process. But, remember that you are Prince Charming, fighting through the brambles of addiction that are keeping you from your beloved goal ... that of living sanely with money.

The sword, in this training program, is your spending plan. But you need lessons in how to effectively use that sword to cut through those brambles. Having a network of other compulsive spenders who understand what you are going through and a program of recovery (whatever that may mean to you) to overcome the addiction are the other two parts of a spiritual triangle that can lead you into the light of sane spending.

So, for now, all I want you to do is to acknowledge Debt as a category. You don't need to list your individual debts right now. This is a big step in itself. I'm really proud of you for having the courage to sit through this lesson. As they say in the U.K., "keep calm and carry on."

In the next lesson, lesson #14, "I'm going to talk about Small Business and Hobby Tax Reporting Made Easy." You can skip this lesson if it doesn't apply to you. But please be sure to listen to lesson #15.

• L E S S O N   # 1 4 •

Small Business and Hobby Tax Reporting Made Easy

BEFORE WE GET INTO MASTER and subcategories for small business tax reporting, I first want to explain how you fold your small business expenses into your spending plan. You can opt to do a completely separate spending plan with just your business master and subcategories. And many advise keeping a wall between your business and personal expenses.

However, if your business is really, really tiny, as is mine, you could opt to just add in the master and subcategories at the bottom of your personal spending plan, which is what I do. In the Master and Subcategories lesson, I talked about using a prefix of TD to differentiate tax deductible items, like TDMedical or TDCharity. So, for business master categories, to differentiate them from my personal master categories, I add the prefix TDBiz. Here is an example:

```
TDBiz-Income
     Income/Royalty Books
     Sales
TDBiz-Advertising
     URLS
     Websites
     Business Cards
TDBiz-Office Expenses
     Postage
     Equipment
     Software
     Supplies
```

SUSAN B.

Create a Tax Subcategory ... and Use It!

I also want to urge you to create a subcategory for federal/state taxes and always subtract the appropriate amount of tax as soon as you receive the income, moving it to the tax category right away. Even if you essentially have a hobby where you make small amounts monthly, or less often, you don't want to be unpleasantly surprised if you end up owing income tax, and then have to scramble to find the money to pay it. I still remember all too painfully well what that was like because I felt it was my right to spend all this money and would tell myself I'll figure it out later! UGH.

So, I think you best consider *this* category sacred, and stay committed not to wipe it out for any other purpose until you've done your taxes and know how much you owe. While I grumble each time I do this, I'm always grateful when I do my taxes. The best situation is that you won't need to pay all that you've withheld and the worst is that you will have the money already put aside so you don't have to worry. It's good to engage in this practice from day one so that when you start earning more money, you're already used to doing this.

Match Your Business Categories to IRS Schedule C Tax Form

If you have any type of small business (including a hobby), you might consider tracking your spending to match the IRS Schedule C tax form categories. Take it from me, this will make it so much easier when it's time to gather your records for your taxes. This lesson contains screen shots and links to helpful sites.

I make small amounts of money on my writing, editing, and book royalties each year. It's enough to qualify as a business if you squint really, really hard. But reporting my deductions when doing my taxes was always so frustrating to me. Gathering the totals and then figuring out which IRS category it fit was time-consuming and annoying.

And then, a few years ago, I realized that all I had to do was create my business categories based on the Schedule C IRS tax categories, so all the appropriate subcategory items were grouped together and could be totaled with ease. Since then, figuring out my deductions at tax time has been a breeze. I'll give you an example in a moment.

Let me explain how I figured this out. First, I looked at the IRS Schedule C expenses list (below). It says, on the top Part II Expenses. But since it may change over time, you may want to go to IRS.gov and search for Schedule C to see a current version. When you do, you'll find a PDF of the actual form and a separate document with instructions on what can be included for each category.

Part II	Expenses. Enter expenses for business use of your home **only** on line 30.					
8	Advertising	8		18	Office expense (see instructions)	18
9	Car and truck expenses (see instructions)	9		19	Pension and profit-sharing plans	19
				20	Rent or lease (see instructions):	
10	Commissions and fees	10		a	Vehicles, machinery, and equipment	20a
11	Contract labor (see instructions)	11		b	Other business property . . .	20b
12	Depletion	12		21	Repairs and maintenance . . .	21
13	Depreciation and section 179 expense deduction (not included in Part III) (see instructions)	13		22	Supplies (not included in Part III)	22
				23	Taxes and licenses	23
				24	Travel, meals, and entertainment:	
14	Employee benefit programs (other than on line 19) . .	14		a	Travel	24a
15	Insurance (other than health)	15		b	Deductible meals and entertainment (see instructions) .	24b
16	Interest:			25	Utilities	25
a	Mortgage (paid to banks, etc.)	16a		26	Wages (less employment credits) .	26
b	Other	16b		27a	Other expenses (from line 48) .	27a
17	Legal and professional services	17		b	**Reserved for future use** . . .	27b

As a writer, many of the IRS categories aren't relevant to me. For instance, I don't have a mortgage, depletion, or depreciation. I have no employees, so I don't have to think about wages, pension, and profit-sharing plans. So, it was easy to know what I didn't need.

But my greatest challenge was trying to understand where my online expenses fit in this list. At the end of this lesson, I've given you some examples of my own subcategories and where I put them. For instance, I found out that costs for my website and URLs go on line 8 Advertising. At the bottom of this lesson, I've included examples to help guide you in choosing how to group your categories. And here's what I've learned. It's really an art, not a science as to how to track online expenses.

My husband and I do our own taxes using TurboTax software [AD FOR TURBOTAX]. In fact, that's where I found most of my answers about how to group my business expenses. I love this software because it actually walks me through category by category to fill in the amounts. Since I organize my subcategories by the IRS Schedule C, it's really simple to total up the master categories and fill in the TurboTax blanks.

But even if I used an accountant, handing over my itemized deductions grouped by the IRS Schedule C categories will make the accountant's job much easier, which could translate into savings on your fee.

If you use TurboTax, you will be able to find many examples as you go through the interview for each type of expense. They also ask about some items individually, and fold these deductions into their appropriate IRS category. Communications, like a cell phone, for example, is, at least, partially deductible if used for business, but I'm not sure which master category it would fit in. So, I made a separate TDBiz-Communications master category with cell phone as a subcategory:

TDBiz-Communications
   TDSusanCellPhone
   TDVOIPPhone

At tax time, I just have my budgeting software generate a report totaling all my business master categories. Then, it's easy to just plug in the total without any hassle.

OK, that's it for tax reporting. If you have any questions or need clarification, please feel free to email me.

Sample of IRS Schedule C Subcategories I Use

Here is a sampling of business subcategories I use in my spending plan. Note that since all my "Biz" categories are tax-deductible, I actually just use the prefix "Biz" without the letters "TD." This still works to differentiate these categories from my personal spending categories.

Biz-Advertising
   Website
   URLs
   Artwork
   Books for promotion
   Business stationery
Biz-OfficeExpenses
   Computer
   Adobe software subscription
   YNAB subscription
   Microsoft Office subscription
   Carbonite backup
   Office supplies
   Postage
   Equipment
   Supplies
   Printer paper/ink
   Small items (cords, tablet cover)

Biz-Communication
- Cell phone
- MagicJack

Biz-Taxes&Licenses
- Bank fees

Biz-Legal&Professional
- TurboTax

Biz-OtherMisc
- P.O. Box
- Ongoing training
- Business books

Biz-Repairs&Maintenance
- Computer
- Tablet
- Phone
- Accessories

Biz-Taxes
- Income tax
- State tax

• LESSON #15 •

Next Step

CONGRATULATIONS ON COMPLETING THIS PORTION of the Fearless Budgeting training. You've done a lot of great work. By now, you should have a pretty complete list of all the places in your life where money goes. This list is going to become the foundation of your spending plan.

Time to Take a Break

I'd like you to pause on the lessons for 24 hours. Just put your list away. Give yourself a break from this work, and allow your subconscious to put its two cents in. Relax and do something that you enjoy that doesn't cost anything - watch some TV, read a book, take a walk, talk to a friend.

After a day of resting from this work, take out your list again. You can add to it, move subcategories to different master categories, or even combine two master categories into one if that's helpful. Or, you may feel satisfied with your list as it is.

I hope, by now, you are feeling more confident, and breathing easier about this process.

This next part is optional. If you have any spending records, like a check register or bank statements, you can skim through them to see if there are any categories you may have missed. For instance, there might be an annual or quarterly bill you hadn't thought about. But there's no pressure to do this. You are perfectly fine to consider your list finished for now.

As I told you at the start, now that you've completed this part of the process, you can come back to this list at any time and move forward. You will never have to start from scratch. You will already have the framework in place, so all you'll have to do is adjust it, and you've had enough practice that it will be easy for you.

At this point, I urge you not to move ahead on your own and fill in any numbers. You'll soon understand why you need to keep from calculating numbers until the right time.

SUSAN B.

How are you feeling? I hope you're encouraged by all the progress you've made. This is a marathon, not a sprint, and taking the time to do this methodically and patiently is calming your adrenalized spending mind. Think of it as decluttering your brain that has been living on rocket fuel around spending.

If you haven't yet done so, I strongly suggest you put in place one or more people to be part of your support network moving forward. It's going to be crucial that you have at least one person who understands what you are accomplishing in this training, why you are doing it, and who will be available to emotionally support you through the process.

Preferably, the people in your network will understand the deadly nature of compulsive spending even if they don't experience it themselves. And it would be best to have someone other than your partner to lean on for support through the rest of the training process.

SECTION III:

COMPLETING THE FRAMEWORK

• LESSON #16 •

Getting Ready for Deeper Water

BEFORE WE BEGIN, LET'S START by taking that long, slow, deep breath in ... breathe out slowly, and let's just sit for a moment.

I hope you realize how far you've come already, and I hope that you're feeling more confident about your ability to move through this process. It's perfectly natural that you are going to experience moments of anxiety and fear, but I hope you've seen that those feelings dissipate as you accomplish each goal. And remember that courage is proceeding on the path despite fear and trepidation.

OK, right now, you have a solid list of master and subcategories that are a snapshot of your life today. That's your foundation.

Now, we need to create a framework on that foundation. And that means dealing with numbers and, eventually, but not yet, a calculator. For those using the spreadsheet, you may not need a calculator at all.

Will You Make Me a Promise?

So, I'm going to ask you to make me a promise. I want you to promise me that you won't add up the numbers in your categories until I tell you to do so. This is a crucial commitment to successfully completing the Fearless Budgeting training. We've waded into the pool by creating your foundation list. But now, we're moving into the deeper water, so it's important to learn how to swim before diving in.

And I also want you to promise me that you will enter into this phase of the training with compassion for yourself. You are doing great work here, and I really want you to practice self-love and compassion as we proceed.

Many of you may be feeling anxiety building as we move into the money side of the training. But again, I'm going to urge you to remember that you are not yet creating a spending plan. Just like we put pen to paper with our list, so, too, are we going to write down numbers. In this part of the training, we're simply looking at numbers on a piece of paper or on a screen ... no totals.

There is no way to create a spending plan until we look clearly and dispassionately at the reality of our spending. Seeing our spending reality is necessary before we can build the spending plan. This is why it's so important to have at least one support person you can turn to who will not judge your spending choices, so that if you start feeling ashamed or berating yourself, your support person can remind you to detach and breathe through the feelings. You need support to walk you through the challenging moments that are coming. But I promise you can overcome every challenge if you just keep moving forward.

There's no judgment, and certainly no shame, about the brave work you're doing. There's no reason to beat yourself up about how much you spend in any category. Again, think of yourself as a detective, putting pieces of a spending puzzle together. Think of all negative thoughts and any desire to run away as just your addict mind feeling threatened by the courageous and healthy changes you are making in your life.

• LESSON #17 •

It's Time to Begin Tracking Your Spending

IN ONE OF THE FIRST LESSONS, the one on why you need a spending plan, I spoke about tracking your numbers. I'm going to repeat a bit of what I said in that lesson:

> *When people say they "track their numbers," it means that every time you buy something, you write down what you bought and how much you spent. It's a necessary component to figuring out the truth about your spending, but it's only the first step in a three-part process and, by itself, it won't give you the truly healing clarity you can have around your spending.*

In this course, we're working backwards, looking at your past spending to develop your spending plan foundation. I think you can now appreciate how keeping track of your spending from now on will make it a lot simpler and easier to know how much you're spending when you actually begin working with your spending plan.

It's very easy to do this, though, at first, it may feel cumbersome and annoying. But those feelings will pass when you see how much this practice helps you. Here's what I suggest:

- You just write down everything you spend and the category it fits in. So, for instance, if you spent $45.33 for a blouse, you would write "$45.33 clothing." You need to be honest and rigorous about tracking your spending to the penny. If you only do it occasionally, or round up, you won't be able to accurately figure out how much you're actually spending in a category.
- When you're out and about, making "brick and mortar" transactions, you can use an app on your phone to write down what you spend. Some people carry a little notebook with them. I kept losing the notebook, so I am very careful to get and keep receipts when I'm out.

However, being imperfect, I'm grateful that I nearly always use my debit card. So, if I forget, or lose, a receipt, I'll be able to check my account online later.

- At home, I have a composition notebook (you know, the one with the marble cover) and I use a different page every day and write down what I've spent and the category. So, if I came home with receipts, I'd just write down the amounts on today's page. If I buy something online, I immediately write it in the book.

Just to share with you more of my own process, I actually write down what I plan to spend each morning as well. And I commit what I plan to spend today as well as what I actually spent yesterday to someone else every day before spending a penny. For me, committing what I spend *before* I spend it is one more way I increase the pause when faced with the impulse to buy. Now, I'm not asking you to do all that. But it is vital that you, at least, write down what you actually spent.

Later, once you have a spending plan, you'll be able to transfer the information from the notebook easily to your spreadsheet or budgeting software or whatever other method you use to manage your spending plan. In this lesson, you can see a picture of one sloppy page in my composition notebook.

1. On the top of the page, I write the date.
2. Then, underneath, on the left side, I write down how much income I plan to receive that day.
3. Under that, I list my planned spending, by category and amount.
4. On the right side, I write down how much I actually spent and, often, where I spent it (in this case, I wrote Publix, which is the name of the grocery store).
5. You'll see a checkmark next to the $29.52. I do that to confirm that I entered the amount into my budgeting software.

So, for instance, I had planned to buy a prescription and committed $38, but I didn't buy it, so I wrote 0 on the right side. Same with the gift. But in a category I call FHP (I group Food, Household, and Personal Care into one master category called FHP), I committed $100 and actually spent $29.52.

FEARLESS BUDGETING

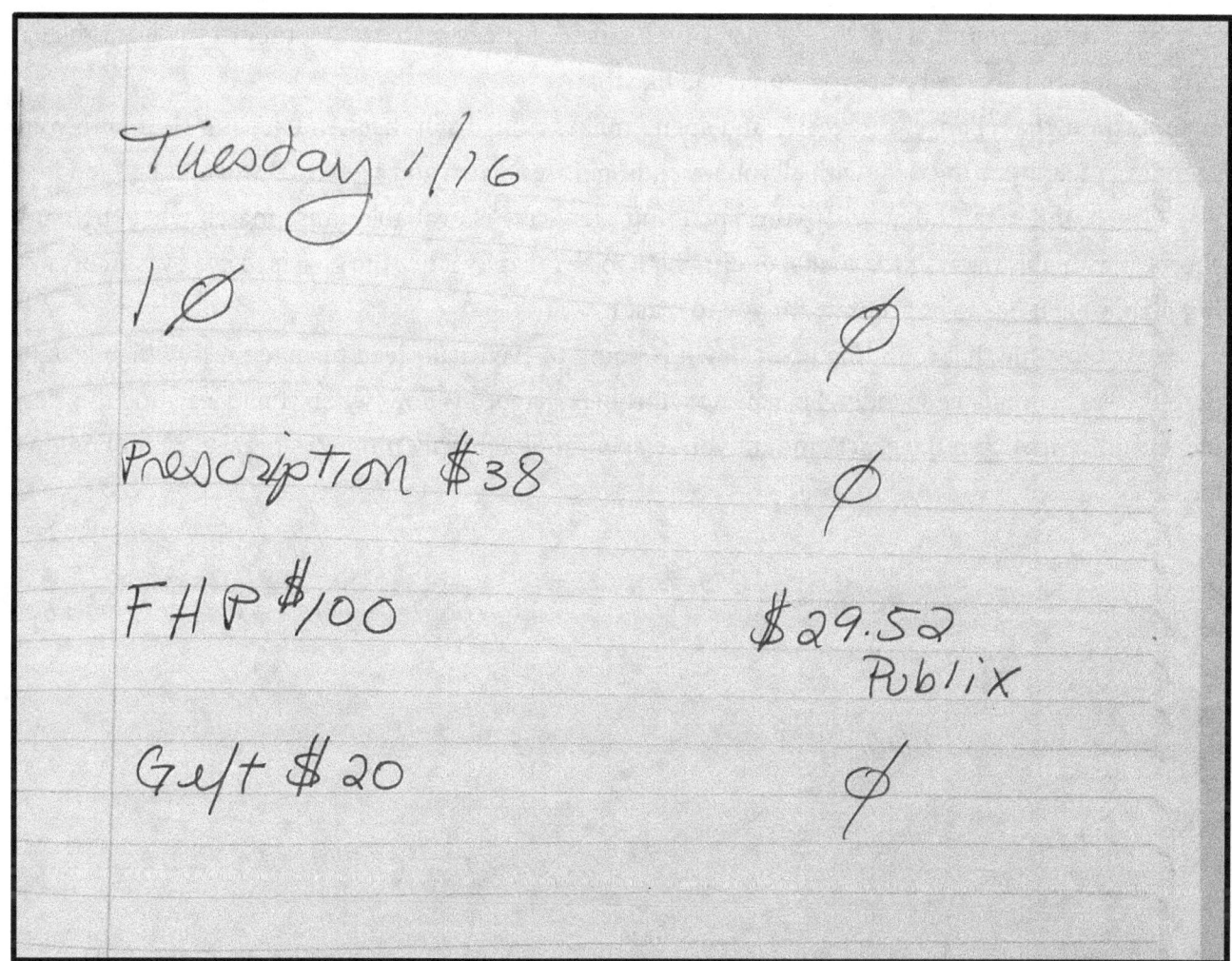

Please don't beat yourself up if you forget to keep track of your spending at first. Nobody is perfect. Your intention is key here. Eventually, it will become second nature for you to capture what you spend, but only if you make the effort to do it when it's not a habit ... until it is. It's really progress, not perfection, when it comes to spending plans. We humans are fallible. I make mistakes all the time with my numbers, transposing them, forgetting to write them down, writing them twice.

Why You Need to Track Your Spending to the Penny

The other point I must impress on you is how important it is to track your spending to the penny. This is a sore spot with many compulsive spenders. The thing is, we want to be clear about our money. And, like it or not, pennies, dimes, nickels, and quarters do make up dollars. Think about it. Would you like it if the bank eliminated the pennies? So, if you get a check for $297.45, they only give you $297.

Or what if a store rounded up? So, for instance, if a pair of shoes costs $89.58, they didn't want to deal with change and charged you $90. Would you like that?

Over time, that change you receive and spend makes a big difference. And getting clear with your spending means getting clear with all your spending. Later, when you are actually using the spending plan, you'll understand that what your spending plan says is available must match what the bank shows as available in order for your spending plan to be reliable. Since the goal is to live by your spending plan, well, it has to be accurate for you to trust it.

Please trust me that rounding up or down is going to eventually lead to vagueness, which is dangerous for a compulsive spender. So, why not start being rigorous now, when you're learning this new habit, and write down the exact amount you're spending? After all, money is precise, why shouldn't we be?

• LESSON #18 •

Detective Work Part I

NOW, WE ARE GOING TO start associating some numbers with your subcategories. But before we do that, we'll be writing some notes in our subcategories. So, we'll start out by using worksheet #2.

In this phase of the training, we're still not going to be looking at income at all. Or any of your debts. We'll talk about those later. Also, please note that this lesson contains a number of screen shots as examples, so you may want to refer to the lesson or the book, if you have it, while listening.

Look for Monthly Bills First

Now, the first thing you are going to do is to go through your list of subcategories, one at a time, and look for any bills that are due monthly, like the electric bill or cable bill. Just write the word "monthly" next to each of those. So, pause the lesson and go do that now.

Find Sporadic Bills

Ok, now, you are going to look through your subcategories again and find bills that you know are due at some other interval. For instance, some bills are just paid once a year (annual) or quarterly (due four times a year) or every six months. Put a note next to each of these to remind you of how often they are paid. If you know what month they are due, write that down as well. For example, "Property Tax – Annual – Due April."

If you are not sure when the bill is next due, don't worry about it for now. Just keep moving forward. You'll be able to come back later to fill in the month they're due. For now, we just want to take care of the easiest entries. So, pause the lesson, and go ahead and fill in what you can.

Alright, great job! You are making excellent progress. Now, we're going to move into the next phase of this lesson and begin to associate some numbers with your subcategories.

If you are using the printed PDF version, you will continue using worksheet #2. If you are using the spreadsheet, you will use worksheet #2A. You'll see that all master and subcategory information has been automatically copied into it.

If You are Paid Weekly

I want to briefly explain the column for weekly totals. This feature is only available in the Excel version of the workbook.

MASTER Category	SUBCATEGORY	Monthly Payment TYPE AMOUNTS	For those paid weekly, here is the weekly amount for each subcategory (Lesson #32) (based on 4 paychecks/month)
Housing	Rent/Mortgage	$500.00	$125.00
	Small Appliances	$10.00	$2.50
	Large Appliances	$25.00	$6.25
	Decorating	$1.00	$0.25
Master Category Total	Repair	$30.00	$7.50
$581.00	Warranties	$15.00	$3.75
	Appliance Service Contracts	$0.00	$0.00
	Pest Control	$0.00	$0.00
	Property Tax - ANNUAL due April	$0.00	$0.00

Special Circumstances begins on line 212. Your additional categories begin on line 262.

I included this in the Excel spreadsheet for people who are paid weekly as an automatic calculation. While I still believe we need to track our spending monthly, those who are paid weekly have a bigger cash flow issue than any other type of pay. In a later lesson. I go into detail about working with a weekly paycheck.

Just ignore this section of the spreadsheet if you are not paid weekly. If you are paid weekly and using the Excel workbook, it will automatically divide the amount you put in your monthly payment by four. (We are not accounting for the occasional fifth paycheck at this time.)

If you are paid weekly, but are using the PDF version of the workbook, you will use a calculator to divide the subcategory monthly amount by four and write it on the associated line (next to each subcategory) in worksheet #2.

In the spreadsheet, you'll also see an area on worksheet #2A to the right of your subcategories where you can enter numbers and the results will be automatically calculated (screenshot a bit later). I will describe how you will use this in a moment. For now, just know that you can type numbers in any of the pink areas and calculations will be automatic.

If you are using the PDF version, you will probably need a calculator at some point, but, again, what I don't want you to do is add up all the numbers in the categories. Remember, you made a commitment not to do that until I tell you to do so. This assignment has nothing to do with getting a total of what you're spending. Right now, that's the last thing you need to know. It's not important.

Ok, now I'm going to give you very clear and explicit instructions on how to proceed. But please wait until I tell you to go ahead before you begin because I guarantee you will get overwhelmed if you jump ahead.

Be Honest and Realistic

You're going to start filling in the subcategories with numbers that reflect the reality of your spending. Reality is the key word here. This is about writing down what you actually spend, not what you think you *should* spend. I totally understand that this could feel stressful for a variety of reasons. I'm definitely taking you out of your comfort zone now, but in this lesson, I'm going to bring you back into it because we're going to start off with the easy stuff.

Remember, at this point, you're still not making a spending plan. You're just capturing reality. Like a snap shot. But I don't mean that you have to know precisely how much you're spending. I just mean that you have to be honest in the numbers you write down. Honesty is the key to succeeding in this part of the training. And remember, each lesson builds on the previous one.

This is *not* the time to judge those numbers or inflict any negative messages on yourself, like "I can't afford this, and I can't do that, and oh no, look how much I spend on that!" No, that's totally counterproductive and the opposite of what we're trying to accomplish in these two lessons!

Think about it this way, you're just capturing information like a dispassionate detective ... or a journalist. That's all you're going to do. This is where you have adjusted your perspective. It's just numbers on paper - tell yourself that it's not a big deal ... because it isn't — you can do this.

Fill in the Easy Stuff

So, how *do* you do this?

Well, you're simply going to go subcategory by subcategory and write down what you think you spend in that subcategory on average each month. I'll talk more about how you figure that out in the next lesson.

For now, we know that there are some subcategories that are simple to fill in because you already know how much you spend on them each month. Those are the ones you just noted with how often you pay the bill, and, if you know, when it's due. For instance, I know I spend $47.95/month on dog insurance, $60.29 on life insurance, $12.99 on dental insurance, and $9.99 on HBO.

So, the first thing I want you to do is to go through your list and write in the amounts that you already know for monthly bills. That should be easy because it's probably all those subcategories you just noted.

Alright, I'd like you to pause the lesson now and go ahead and do that.

That was simple, right? Not difficult at all. Great job. Your confidence will increase with each subcategory you fill in.

A Crucial Fearless Budgeting Concept (and Periodic Bills)

So, let's move on. Now, let's talk about bills that are due at another interval. You know, the ones you just noted are due quarterly, annually, every six months, etc. I'm about to explain a crucial Fearless Budgeting concept that is key to making this system work for you.

What we're going to do is figure out how much we want to allocate monthly to bills that are due less often. Here's an example, and then, I'm going to tell you exactly how to do this yourself.

Let's take my dog license subcategory.

I pay my $15 dog license annually. So, in order to figure out how much I have to allocate monthly, I will divide $15/12 months = $1.25 per month. I need to accumulate $1.25/month to be able to pay my dog license each year. I'm going to talk a lot more about why this is the best practice for compulsive spenders later on, but it should be clear that allocating $1.25/month toward my dog license is a lot less painful than scrambling to find $15 when the license is due.

Let me give you another example. I know that I pay for a rabies certificate every three years. It's $19. I divide $19/36 months and that equals 53 cents. Again, a lot easier to put away 53 cents than to find $19.

And if you think that seems ridiculous, think about the fact that there are probably lots of these types of bills you have. So, it may be 53 cents here and $1.25 there, but it could be a lot more when you think about *all* the expenses you have. So, you may not feel like saving up for three years, but **I would urge you to follow this practice for bills due annually or more often.**

OK, so how to figure out these amounts. If you are using the spreadsheet, just type the **total amount** of the bill you pay each time anywhere in the calculation area in one of the pink cells. On the next page, there's a screenshot of the work area with a number ($2,500) typed into one of the pink cells (to be calculated). See the screenshot on the next page.

- "3-month average" is the second block
- "Due Annually" is the third block
- "Due Quarterly" is the fourth block
- "Due every 6 months" is the fifth block

The spreadsheet automatically calculates the amount to type into the "Monthly Payment" field for the associated subcategory. Note: You will not need the gold area (second block from the left) for this lesson. But you'll use it in the next lesson.

MASTER Category	SUBCATEGORY	Monthly Payment	Notes and Tips (If paid weekly, divide by 4 and put total here. - see Lesson #22)
Debt Repayment			
	Copy information from Worksheet #3		
	Master Category Total	Write the amount from Worksheet #3, Total Monthly Payments, under Master Category Total	

Skip categories not relevant to you.

- "3-month average" is the second block
- "Due Annually" is the third block
- "Due Quarterly" is the fourth block
- "Due every 6 months" is the fifth block

The spreadsheet automatically calculates the amount to type into the "Monthly Payment" field for the associated subcategory. Note: You will not need the gold area (second block from the left) for this lesson. But you'll use it in the next lesson.

| DUE ANNUALLY (every 12 months): | $208.33 | Type this number into the **Monthly Payment** for the subcategory. |

For the monthly amount for a bill due annually (once a year), look at the green section. In this case, the total of $2,500 is divided by 12, so the number to type into the "Monthly Payment" field for the subcategory is $208.33.

| DUE QUARTERLY (4 times a year): | $833.33 | Type this number into the **Monthly Payment** for the subcategory. |

For the monthly amount for a bill due quarterly (due four times a year), look at the blue section. In this case, the total of $2,500 is divided by three, so the number to type into the "Monthly Payment" field is $833.33.

| DUE every 6 months: | $416.67 | Type this number into the **Monthly Payment** for the subcategory. |

For the monthly amount for a bill due every six months, look at the black section. In this case, the total of $2,500 is divided by six, so the number to type into the "Monthly Payment" field is $416.67.

Quarterly Bills

I want to explain more about quarterly bills because even I find this confusing. Quarterly bills are paid four times a year. Quarterly bills are paid four times a year. Let's use quarterly taxes as an example because that is pretty straightforward. The bill is due on:

- January 15th
- April 15th
- July 15th
- October 15th.

Where it gets confusing is how to accumulate for this. It's due four times a year, but you need to save up for it over three months. For example, let's say you owe $900 each quarter.

- If you divide the total you pay by three, you will consistently have the money to pay the tax bill.
- In this case, each month will be funded with $300.
- So, for instance, you will fund the money for July's bill in:
    - April
    - May
    - June

In practical terms, this means that in the month the bill is due (July, in this case), you will have accumulated $1,200 in the category. After you pay the $900 bill, you'll still have the July amount of $300 that goes toward October's payment.

If you are still unclear about this, please email me or post a question in the student discussion forum so I can explain it further.

PDF Instructions and More Clarification

If you are using the PDF version of the workbook, you will need to use a calculator to figure out the monthly number. It's really easy to do. You just divide the amount of the bill you pay each time by the number of months between each payment.

If you do have periodic bills, now is the time to grab your calculator, so go ahead and get it now.

Let's say I pay $500 every six months for car insurance. I would just divide 500/6. The monthly number is $83.33. Then, I'd write that amount next to car insurance. Or, maybe I pay $1,200 for estimated taxes quarterly. I would divide $1,200/3, which equals $400. Then, I would write $400 in the monthly payment category.

Now let's say I pay my water bill quarterly. This is a bit more complicated because it will not be the same amount each time. Let's hold off on anything that is not always going to be the same payment until the next lesson.

Bills Due Sooner than Usual

I just want to mention one more important variation on your bill payments. It's also likely that one or more of these periodic bills will be due sooner than expected based on when you are doing this training. For instance, an annual bill due in December would normally give you 12 months to accrue. But if you are creating your spending plan foundation in October, then you would actually have to pay it in three months, not 12.

For now, don't worry about that. I will address that in Course #2 Working with Your Spending Plan in lesson #7.

Remember, I asked you to write a note stating what month these bills are due. But, for the purpose of creating your spending plan **foundation**, you want to base the amount you write in on what would happen in the normal course of your life. So, in the case of an annual bill, for instance, since you would normally have 12 months to accumulate money for the bill, you would still divide it by 12 and put in the result as your monthly allocation for that subcategory.

So, now, why don't you go ahead and continue working on filling in the monthly bill amounts that you know off the top of your head as well as calculating and entering those that are not monthly (but where you know the total due). In the next lesson, we'll talk about how to fill in the rest of your subcategories.

LESSON #19

Detective Work Part II

BY NOW YOU'VE FILLED IN some of the blanks in your list with numbers. I hope you can see this really isn't as hard as you thought, is it? But now, we're going into more challenging territory. It may be a good idea to begin this process on the phone with somebody you trust to support and encourage you until you see how easy this is to do and you feel more confident about it.

Notice in the last lesson that I said you're going to write down "what you *think* you spend," because if you haven't been keeping track of your spending, how would you know? Well, you guess. You take your best guess.

But, if you *do* have any records of your spending, like a check register or bank statements, I definitely want you to use them to get a sense of what you've spent over time. You don't need a calculator for this part of the process. And if you don't have any available records, it's no problem.

Let me talk about how to guesstimate first if you have no records, and then I'll go through how to use bank statements (or a check register). Whether you guess or work with bank statements, this process is going to take some time. You may want to bookend, letting someone know when you start working on this and commit to doing it for a specified period of time, like 10 or 20 minutes, and then let them know that you've completed your commitment.

I've had students who wanted to just rip off the band-aid and launched in, spending hours all at once to get this done. Other people have taken a few days to work through the list. This can be a moment that may make you want to bail out of the Fearless Budgeting course. Please turn to your support system to help you remember why you're doing this and to help you stay motivated despite your anxiety, boredom, annoyance, whatever the feeling. This is not going to take much time in the scheme of your life. And once it's done, I promise you're going to feel an enormous sense of relief and accomplishment.

Don't forget to pause and do your calming breath throughout this process.

And again, if you're using the PDF version of the workbook, you'll be entering information into worksheet #2. If you're using the spreadsheet, you'll be using worksheet #2A.

Guessing

If you have no available records, then you are going to look at each subcategory and give it no more than a minute or two to think about how much you spend monthly in that category. My experience is that compulsive spenders inevitably underestimate their spending. I also think your first guess is most accurate. So, I would take that guess and add 10% to it. And that's the number to write down. So, if I guess that I spend $750 on food each month, I'm going to add 10% to that (which is $75) and write $825 next to food.

As I keep saying, these numbers are not written in stone. We're still just building the framework on the foundation to create a spending plan.

And for everyone, whether or not you use a bank statement to figure out your spending, **if there is a category that you want to fund, but are not yet able to do so, put $1 in that category as a placeholder to set your intention.**

For instance, maybe you want to take a class or get a massage or go on vacation or learn how to paint. Notice, I'm not talking about "saving up" for this, I'm talking about **funding** these categories. It's a subtle, but important difference.

By allocating all your money, every penny, to a category, you are creating a map of how your money will be spent over time. It's vastly different from the white-knuckle approach of completely depriving yourself in other categories to "save up" for what you want or scrambling to find the money when you decide to buy something or when a bill is due.

> *Here's a thought about your vacation category. You may want to create a mini-spending plan around a specific vacation. Now, you should already have subcategories set up. But it's wise to add a category for unexpected expenses when on vacation, and then fund that subcategory with an additional 10% of your vacation fund. In other words, if all the costs for flight, hotel, car, food, entertainment, etc., come to $1,200, if possible, add another $120 for unexpected expenses.*

You will discover that when you begin to live by your categories and allocate your money in a balanced way, long-term categories for wants will organically grow because you've responsibly planned for needs and allowed yourself some short-term wants as well. If your financial situation is extremely tight, that is where your network and a recovery program will help you to adjust your wants one day at a time. In the end, it's all about choices, a topic I'm going to talk about at great length in a future lesson.

Using Bank Statements

Now, if you have bank statements, print out three full months' worth. So, if it's November when you are taking the Fearless Budgeting training course, you'll print out August, September, and October, Certainly, you can print out additional earlier months later if you'd like even more clarity, but three months is plenty to begin with. We want to keep this process manageable and not overwhelming. But please listen to this entire lesson to give yourself time to understand the process before engaging in it.

Remember that any time you start to feel anxious, you can stop the lesson, take that long, slow, deep centering breath, let it out slowly, and just sit in the pause. And hopefully, you can make a call to someone to talk about how you're feeling if the discomfort persists.

You're going to look through these bank statements to figure out how much you've spent in the rest of your subcategories. But before you do, let me explain how to do this. First of all, just a reminder to ignore any subcategories in the workbook that aren't relevant to you. You can delete them from the Excel workbook in worksheet #2. Or just draw a line through them if you have the PDF version. Also, if you are using the PDF version of the workbook, you will need a piece of paper or two to use as a notepad to list transactions. This will make sense in a moment.

What you are going to do is go category by category and look for transactions that fit into those categories. So, you'll look at each transaction on your bank statement one by one, and then write the amount down. It doesn't matter which statement you begin with.

Please do not do anything with income. We're only looking at spending transactions. And wait on any debt repayment as well.

So, if you are using the Excel spreadsheet, first, just type each transaction for the category you are working on in the notepad area of the workbook (any of the pink cells in columns H to Z as I described in the previous lesson). If you are using the PDF version, you will write down this transaction amount on your notepad.

Then, put a check mark, highlight, or scratch through the transaction on your bank statement so you know you've accounted for it. Here is a screenshot:

02/28/2018	Credit Interest	$4.65	$3,290.52
02/28/2018	POS Withdrawal VERVANTE CORPORATI 650-x7000 UTUS	($21.87)	$3,285.87
02/28/2018	POS Withdrawal PALMS WEST HOSPITA 561-798-1733 TNUS	($32.00)	$3,307.74
02/28/2018	POS Withdrawal MIGHTYTEXT HTTPSMIGHTYTECAUS	($5.94)	$3,339.74
02/26/2018	SUSAN BILHEIMER - P2P PAYMNT	$2,000.00	$3,345.68
02/26/2018	POS Withdrawal CMX-WELLINGTON RET WELLINGTON FLUS	($12.84)	$1,345.68
02/26/2018	POS Withdrawal WHOLEFDS WLL 10195 WELLINGTON FLUS	($16.48)	$1,358.52
02/25/2018	POS Withdrawal WAL-MART #6967 Wal-Mart Super Cen LAKE WORTH FLUS	($42.71)	$1,375.00

In this example, I am doing this exercise in March, so I begin by looking at spending in February. I am looking for all food transactions. In this case, I found three so far. So, I typed them in the notepad area of the Excel workbook and highlighted them in the bank statement (above).

You can see in the screenshot on the next page that I typed $12.84, $42.71, and $16.48. Then, in the gold section above (in the print version, the second block from the left), you can see that the numbers are automatically added up and divided by three to give you a monthly average. At the moment, the monthly average is $24.01. But since I have only gone through one month, I wouldn't yet type that amount in the food subcategory. I would do that after entering all the food transaction amounts for the three months. Don't worry, there are 76 pink cells into which you can type transactions.

Use the pink area, below, to type in up to 76 transactions for a specific subcategory. *Scroll to the right to see the additional cells.* (See Lessons #18 and #19 for further explanation)	3 month average:	$24.01	Type this number into the **Monthly Payment** for the subcategory.			
$12.84	$42.71					
$16.48						

Once you've gone through all three months, then, you will take the three-month average number and type it into the Food subcategory. If you are using the PDF version, you will add up all the transactions for that subcategory that you have written down and divide that total by three.

Now that we're talking about this category, I'm sure you won't know the breakdown of food vs. house supplies vs. personal care. That is OK because they are all contained within one master category called Groceries.

You might consider putting 80% of that three-month average into Food, 10% into House Supplies, and 10% into Personal Care. But you can always just put it all into Food for now or just pick an amount to put into each. I'll talk more about this in a few minutes.

It doesn't have to be perfect, but it's a solid start.

You'll take one subcategory at a time. So, when you've found all the transactions for one subcategory for the three months, take the three-month average (divide the total by three), and entered the number next to the subcategory. Then, you will go on to the next subcategory. If you're using the Excel version, don't forget to erase all the numbers in the pink notepad section of the Excel workbook before going on to the next subcategory.

If you only have transactions in one month for a subcategory, that's fine, but you'll still put the three-month average as the monthly number to accumulate for now. Here's an example. Let's say you spent $450.87 on clothing in one month, but nothing in the other two months. I would still say to take the three-month average ($450.87/3), which is $150.29, and enter it next to the Clothing subcategory for now. You can always adjust it later.

Our Goal is to Run on Automatic

The Fearless Budgeting attitude is to keep your spending plan smooth and balanced. That means we do our best to accumulate in subcategories over time using the same amount in the subcategory month after month, so we don't have to suddenly remember to allocate money when we need it.

For compulsive spenders, the more we can make this a passive process where you don't get your adrenaline going or have to dwell on figuring out where to get the money for a purchase, the more comfortable we will be in the long run with our spending plan and the more likely we will stick with it.

Once you've finished going through all three bank statements and all your subcategories, most transactions on the statement will be highlighted/scratched through, other than income, refunds, or other money that came *into* your account, and your debt payments.

However, there may be some stragglers, that you aren't sure where they fit in. That's OK. Sometimes, it is simple to figure out. For instance, if you bought something from an online store, such as Amazon, it's easy to look at your orders to see what you bought. If it is obvious what subcategory it fits, then, divide by three to get the three-month average and add it to the number you already wrote down for that subcategory.

In this case, even if you are using the Excel workbook, you will need a calculator to add the number to the amount you already typed into the subcategory. For instance, let's take the clothing example again. We used the monthly average of $150.29, but later, we found another $9 purchase for clothing: $9/3=3. So, we change the monthly average to $153.29.

QUESTIONS

Before we move on, I am anticipating two questions:

1. What do I do if I'm not sure what subcategory a transaction fits in?
   And
2. What do I do if one transaction covers multiple subcategories?

Let's start with the first question. If you aren't sure what subcategory a transaction fits in, either create a new subcategory somewhere for that type of spending or just pick the closest subcategory that you think would fit for now. This isn't written in stone, so you can always change it later. They key is not to keep moving forward and not to get stuck on such details.

Now, for #2, how do we handle a transaction that covers multiple categories? For instance, at the pharmacy, let's say I bought a prescription and paper towels. We call that a split transaction because prescriptions and paper towels would fit into different subcategories, so I want you to get used to that term. If one transaction fits multiple categories, either take your best guess at how much goes into each category or just pick a single category. I truly don't want you to stress out about it. This is an art, not a science. No one is grading you.

Remember, I addressed this earlier when I spoke about grocery store transactions, where you may buy food and also house supplies. At this point, it's really fine to put it all into the Food subcategory for now, and just put $1 as a placeholder in the House Supplies subcategory. You'll have lots of time later, when you're actually working with your spending plan and tracking your spending, to see how much of that money is going to house supplies vs. food. It's not important right now.

So, please don't give more than 30 seconds to a minute maximum thinking about what category a transaction belongs in. Truly, you are still just building the framework. And there are no category police looking over your shoulder. When you're done, you should have an amount in every subcategory in your foundational document (that's the workbook), even if it's just $1.

I realize this may be stretching your willingness to be uncomfortable to its limits. Take breaks and make calls to get support. It is not endless, though it may seem interminable when you begin. But when you are finished, you are going to be amazed at how good having this degree of clarity around your spending feels. This is no time to judge. It's just time to continue putting together the puzzle pieces of your spending.

If you have debt, a lesson is coming up soon where you will complete that part of the process.

It's time to put your workbook away for now. But please keep the bank statements to use if they include any debt payments or if you need help figuring out your income. Give yourself a day to settle down around this. It's exhausting and stressful. But you'll never have to do this level of detective work again if you keep moving forward now. You are getting so close to having a spending plan. And it **will** be worth it in the end.

Again, I hope you feel really proud of all the work you've done and your willingness to keep going despite your discomfort. You are building recovery muscles by doing this work ... gaining strength to say no to your bullying addict mind, embracing your developing spending plan, and making it part of your life.

After you've let yourself relax for a day or so, I'll see you in the next lesson.

• LESSON #20 •

Add Up the Numbers on the Worksheet

HOPEFULLY, YOU'RE FEELING REFRESHED AND ready to take the next step in developing your spending plan.

You only have a few more lessons to complete before you have your spending plan foundation. You've come so far. Please keep moving forward. Think about Prince Charming and that Sword of Truth. You are in the brambles now. You have been training. You are going to slice right through those brambles and slay any dragons that you face to get to your goal.

Let's take a moment and do our calming breath here. Take that deep breath in and let it out. Then pause.

We're now going to address the totals in each master category, which are made up of all your subcategories ... other than debt. If you have debt, the next lesson is devoted to addressing that subject. Just let it go for now.

If you are using the Excel workbook, the master category totals have been automatically calculated for you. You will see them underneath the master category name in the green area (under "Master Category Total"). There is a screenshot on the next page.

In this example, you can see that the monthly total of all subcategories in Housing is $581. If you are using the PDF version of the workbook, you will need a calculator to total up all the monthly payments and write it in.

I also want you to note that I only put $1 in Decorating. That's because I don't currently have the money to fund this subcategory but hope to be able to do so eventually. You'll also notice that I deleted three subcategories that appear in your copy of the workbook that I didn't need - Appliance Service Contracts, Pest Control, and Property Tax. So, again, feel free to clean up this workbook by eliminating subcategories you don't need.

MASTER Category	SUBCATEGORY	Monthly Payment TYPE AMOUNTS
Housing	Rent/Mortgage	$500.00
	Small Appliances	$10.00
	Large Appliances	$25.00
	Decorating	$1.00
Master Category Total	Repair	$30.00
$581.00	Warranties	$15.00

Don't worry about making a mistake. This is very much a work-in-progress right now. By the time you actually have a spending plan and are ready to use it, numbers aren't going to scare you anymore. You'll feel in charge of them, instead of feeling that they are controlling you.

Reminder - All of this is not yet your real spending plan. You are still just capturing what you actually spend on paper, to the best of your ability, so it reflects reality. At this point, please don't lower any subcategory amounts just because you're afraid you're spending too much in a given category. The point of our work right now is for you to see reality clearly, not to delude yourself, beat yourself up, or judge yourself. You're defeating the purpose if you do that.

The key here, and why you have to take the heat out of it and stop to breathe and relax, is that you have to see that facing reality is not going to hurt you. So, just write down what you really spend or, if guessing, guess 10% higher. They're just numbers on paper or a screen. Still, nowhere near a spending plan yet.

So, if you're using the PDF version of the workbook, calculate your numbers now, and fill in the worksheet. If you're using the Excel workbook, totals are automatically calculated. I'll see you in the next lesson if you have debt. Otherwise, you can skip to the Time to Talk Income lesson that follows.

• L E S S O N   # 2 1 •

For Those with Debt

THIS LESSON IS JUST FOR those who have debt. If you don't have debt, congratulations! Please go on to the next lesson.

But for those who do have debt, let me just talk to you about an extra step I'm going to ask you to take. For you, this lesson is going to be challenging. I know from personal experience how uncomfortable it will be to do what I'm going to ask you to do. And it may not be possible for you to complete this lesson in one or two sessions, depending on your situation. That's OK. At least you can get the process started.

But don't forget why you are going through the Fearless Budgeting training. It's to become unafraid of reality around your spending and willing to live in reality ongoing.

Let me start by saying that your creditors are not your boss. You do not have to live in abject deprivation in order to pay off your creditors. In fact, the reality may be that you can pay only $5/month or even nothing at all, if your situation is dire enough, no matter how large your debt.

Remember that you have a right to live a balanced life. And you are not your debts. You are taking an enormous step to become responsible and accountable for your spending. And that is noble.

So, the fact of what you can realistically afford to pay your creditors may be vastly different from even the minimum amount they expect you to pay monthly ... or the additional amount you may feel driven to pay.

Again, I urge you to remember that we are just writing down numbers.

In this lesson, we will be using worksheet #3 (also located at the end of this lesson). You will want to get your bank statements if you have been making payments. I will talk about other options for discovering your debt information in a few minutes. If you are working with the PDF version of the workbook, you will want to use a pencil with an eraser to enter the information because amounts will change, and you will want to keep this sheet updated.

I suggest that you use this worksheet for unsecured debts, like credit cards and lines of credit, since you're likely listing secured loans, such as your mortgage or car payment, in their own subcategories. A secured loan means that there's something of equal value that the creditor can take if you default on the loan.

You've done a great job on filling in your subcategories. That was a lot of intensive work, and I applaud you for doing so. But now, you have to go even further. And for this, I strongly advise getting support because it will take tremendous courage if you have been avoiding facing the reality of your debt.

Let's first deal with any debts you are currently paying off. You may want to look through your three months of bank statements to find these debt payments.

1. First, put the month and year you created this Debt worksheet in the space next to Today's Date.
2. Enter the name of the creditor (such as Chase Bank Visa Card).
3. Enter the amount you pay monthly in the Monthly Minimum Due field. If you aren't sure if your payment is more or less than the minimum payment, make a note to remind yourself to find out the true minimum amount due later.
4. Since you are making this payment monthly, put a check mark or type "Y" in the "P?" Field (this stands for "paying").
5. You can come back to the Total Owed and Interest Rate later.

So, pause this lesson to enter in the information from your records.

Once you have done this ... well ... breathe first. I know this is hard. But I'm telling you that it's vital that you face the truth. There's no way around it. You have to go through it. But if you keep moving forward, you will eventually reach the other side, and you will feel more peaceful. Really.

Now, once you have those debts listed, I suggest you try to go into their associated online accounts to find out and fill in the minimum monthly due, total owed, and interest rate. If you can't access the information online, then, we'll talk about other ways to get the information later.

You can pause this lesson and come back to it once you've done this.

After you complete the work on debts you are currently paying off, or at least as far as you can get, it's time to seek out the rest of your debts. Take a break if necessary, but please come back to this. Just think about how far you've come.

This is the time to gather together all the mail from creditors you haven't opened ... and open them. You probably want to sort them by debt and then by date, so you can throw out all but the most recent statements or other information.

You may want to look at your credit report to find debts you don't remember. In the Fearless Budgeting Resources, I've put a link to the Federal Trade Commission website that has a link for you to get your free credit report. So, you know it's a legitimate website.

Write or type in the information about each debt into worksheet. For debts on which you aren't currently making monthly payments at this time, just enter "N" in the P? Column.

Once you've put in this preliminary information, you're going to embark on more detective work:

1. It is important that you find out and write down the monthly minimum due on all your debts. You should be able to find this information without having to call your creditor, either from the online account or a statement you may have received.
2. Write down the interest rate on the worksheet. You can usually find that in your account online or in the monthly statement.
3. Finally, for all your debts, find out the total due on each one and write that in. I know this must feel terrifying, but you have to do it if you want to get clear.

Once you've finished, if you are using the Excel workbook, the calculations have been done and all this information has been added to worksheet #2A.

MASTER Category	SUBCATEGORY	Monthly Payment	Notes and Tips (If paid weekly, divide by 4 and put total here. - see Lesson #22)
Debt Repayment			
	Copy information from Worksheet #3	Write the amount from Worksheet #3, Total Monthly Payments, under Master Category Total	
Master Category Total			

Skip categories not relevant to you.

For the PDF Version Only

If you are using the PDF version of the workbook, you'll do the following:

1. Add up all the minimum monthly payments for your debts to come up with a grand total and write that next to the "Total Monthly." (That will be a theoretical amount that you would pay each month for all your debts if you were paying all the minimum payments. Remember, this is not necessarily your reality. It's just a snapshot.)
2. Add up the total amount owed and write that number next to where it says "Total Owed" on the top of the debt worksheet.
3. Once you are done, just write the total monthly amount in worksheet #2 in the Debts section (under the "Master Category Total"). There is a screen shot on the following page where the Master Category Total is circled.

I know this could feel like a very demoralizing exercise, and it may take enormous energy, effort, and some time to gather this information. That's OK.

I'm sure this feels overwhelming and very scary right now. I understand that you may not want to speak with your creditors at this time, so just do your best to gather this information from your account online, statements, or the free credit report you order.

Please don't brush this off, because moving into the light around all your spending, including your debts, is integral to your success.

We have to rip the band-aid off of your denial and this is the only way to do it. You'll want to keep this sheet because when you actually create your spending plan, you'll be making choices about which debts you can make payments on and how much to pay on each, so your total monthly debt payment will most likely change from the number you see right now.

Cry if you need to, rail at the universe, call someone and vent. But please, don't let this keep you from the goal that you are so close to reaching. And please, please, please, don't use this an excuse to tell yourself that your situation is hopeless, so you might as well spend.

It's not hopeless. I tell you again that I paid off $34,000 of debt despite becoming disabled and losing half my income. I tell you that miracles can happen if you get willing to change. But the miracle definitely won't happen if you run away from the truth.

Next, we're going to move into figuring out your income. If you need a day or so to regain your balance, that's fine. But please don't give up now. You have done most of the hard work. And you can proceed with the rest of the training while you continue to work on this lesson.

WORKSHEET #3 DEBT WORKSHEET

Total Monthly Payment:

Total Debt Owed:

Today's Date:

NOTES	Name of Card or Debt	Monthly Minimum Due	Total Owed	Interest rate
				%
				%
				%
				%
				%
				%
				%
				%
				%
				%
				%
				%
				%
				%
				%
				%
				%
				%
				%
				%
				%
				%
				%
				%
				%
				%

END OF DEBT WORKSHEET

• LESSON #22 •

Time to Talk Income

IT'S NOW TIME TO FIGURE out your income. There are three basic types of income:

1. **Regular income**
   Regular income includes your paycheck, business income, disability payments, social security, alimony, child support, tenant rent. It would also include what you earn in your primary occupation as a freelancer, consultant, coach, etc. This is the money you live on day to day.
2. **Sporadic Income**
   The second type of income is sporadic income, and that would include a tax refund, yard sale, eBay, craft fair profit, bonus, etc.
3. **Windfalls**
   Finally, there are windfalls, which include birthday checks, inheritance, money found in the street, winning the lottery.

But what about monthly interest or dividends you receive as part of your income? Well, we're talking here about only listing money that you can spend. So, for instance, if you don't actually receive a check for stock dividends, but they get reinvested, then you won't list it on this worksheet.

If you receive interest, it may not be the same month after month. I would leave it out for now if it's not substantial and it varies month to month. Otherwise, put in the current amount of interest you receive monthly in the Monthly Income Source.

You will be working with worksheet #4 (also located at the end of this lesson). The only income we are going to include in our spending plan foundation is regular income. If you're using the Excel workbook, you will type in the monthly income source and amount, and you will see the total income automatically calculated. If you are using the PDF version, you will add up all your monthly income and enter it in the space for "Total Income."

I have also included a place to note the source of any sporadic income you can think of and any windfalls you typically or potentially receive. You can include an average amount you receive and how often.

While I've asked you to dig in to look for all sources of income, we're not going to be doing anything else with windfalls or sporadic income for now. But it's important for you to have this information when you begin working with your spending plan. Right now, we are making a spending plan foundation based on money you receive monthly. I'll talk about self-employed, contract, and commission-based workers in a moment.

Now, on to regular pay or income. If you are a full or part-time employee at a company where they take out taxes, 401K, medical, etc., the paycheck amount I want you to consider is the actual amount you receive, also called the net, not the amount before withholding is taken out, which is called the gross amount.

I'm going to go through a number of scenarios and help you figure out how much you earn monthly. Please note that if you are using the Excel workbook, all of these calculations are done for you automatically.

For Those Using the Excel Workbook

If you're using the Excel workbook, you will just type in the amount for one paycheck in the pink area under "How to Calculate Your Paycheck for the Monthly Amount" for the area relevant to the type of pay you receive, such as weekly, bi-weekly (every two weeks), or semi-monthly (twice a month). Then, type in the calculated "Monthly Amount" in the "Amount Received Monthly" column next to the source for the pay. Here's a sample screenshot:

WORKSHEET #4 INCOME WORKSHEET			TOTAL:	$1,600.00	
Monthly Income Source	Amount Received Monthly		How to Calculate Your Paycheck for the Monthly Amount (See Lesson #22)		
Paycheck - (not including two extra checks a year)	$1,600.00				
			Paid Weekly	One paycheck x 4	*(Counting five week months)* One paycheck x 52 / 12
			Type one paycheck amount	Monthly Amount $0.00	Monthly Amount $0.00
			Paid Bi-Weekly (every two weeks)	One paycheck x 2	*(Counting the two extra checks)* One paycheck x 26 / 12
			Type one paycheck amount $800.00	Monthly Amount $1,600.00	Monthly Amount $1,733.33

In this case, I get paid every two weeks. So, I typed in $800, which is the amount for one paycheck, into the Paid Bi-Weekly (every two weeks) pink cell. It gave me a monthly amount based on two paychecks and a monthly amount counting the two extra paychecks I receive a year.

I chose to use the smaller number to be comfortable knowing I will definitely get this amount monthly. So, I typed $1,600 next to the income source Paycheck. And notice in the screenshot that I added a note about this next to the Source, stating, "Paycheck - not including two extra checks a year."

Calculating Monthly Pay from a Second Job

Now, I need to figure out the monthly amount for the paycheck from my second job.

Note: If you have more than one source of pay, be sure to delete the number you previously typed into the "How to Calculate Your Paycheck for the Monthly Amount" form. Then, type in the amount for one paycheck for the next source.

WORKSHEET #4 INCOME WORKSHEET		TOTAL:		$2,400.00
Monthly Income Source	Amount Received Monthly	How to Calculate Your Paycheck for the Monthly Amount (See Lesson #22)		
Paycheck - (not including two extra checks a year)	$1,600.00			*(Counting five week months)*
2nd job - weekly (I didn't count extra paychecks)	$800.00	Paid Weekly	One paycheck x 4	One paycheck x 52 / 12
		Type one paycheck amount $200.00	Monthly Amount $800.00	Monthly Amount $866.67

I typed $200, the amount of one paycheck, in the "Paid Weekly" pink cell. And, again, I chose to use the number calculated for only four checks a month. I typed $800 into the "Amount Received Monthly" column next to the second job income source. Again, I added a note that I didn't count the extra paychecks.

For Those Using the PDF Workbook

Now, if you are using the PDF version of the workbook, here are instructions:

Paid Weekly

If you get paid weekly, there are two ways to account for your monthly pay.

- You could multiply one week's paycheck by 52.
- Then divide that number by 12 to get a monthly amount.

However, that will create a more severe cash flow problem until you receive that fifth paycheck. Depending on when you are creating your spending plan foundation, that could be months from now.

So, for purposes of this lesson:

- I strongly suggest that you multiply one paycheck by four, which is the number of paychecks you'll receive for most months.
- Factor in the extra paychecks later, when you receive them.
- I would also make a note next to the source that you will get an extra paycheck occasionally. See the screen shots above.

Paid Bi-Weekly (Every Two Weeks)

For those who get paid every two weeks, also called bi-weekly, that means you get 26 paychecks a year. Most months you'll receive two checks, but twice a year, you receive a third check.

As with the weekly pay, there are two ways to figure this out:

- Multiply one paycheck amount by 26 and divide by 12.
- Or, my strong suggestion is to ignore those occasional extra checks for now other than making a note about them, and just add up two checks and write that amount in.

Paid Semi-Monthly (Twice a Month)

If you get paid twice a month, which is also called semi-monthly (for instance, on the 15th and 30th), then just add up two paychecks to get the monthly amount.

Paid Monthly

For workers who are paid once a month, or if you receive, for instance, SSDI or social security, a pension, alimony, or any other regular monthly payment, simply list that monthly amount on the worksheet in the "Amount Received Monthly" column next to the income source.

If you are not an hourly or salaried employee, but, instead, work on commission, bonus, freelance, or another irregular payment schedule, the best thing to do is to:

1. Look at your last year's total net income.
2. Then, divide that number by 12. That gives you an average you make in a month.
3. However, I also suggest that you also note in the "Monthly Income Source" column the lowest and highest monthly amount you earned in the last year. That will be valuable information later.

Regarding sporadic income, say you sell items on Etsy or eBay, sell art or jewelry, receive book royalties, or do side work, just enter some information about it in the Sporadic Income Source area. Here is an example:

Sporadic Income Source	Windfalls You Receive
Ebay - $25 last month, $400 in January, $28 in December	
Tax refund	
Book royalties - average is $30/month	

Totaling Up Your Income

If you're using the Excel version of the workbook, all the calculations will be done for you, so you can move on to the next lesson once you've entered monthly amounts for all your income sources. If you are using the PDF version of the workbook, please go ahead and add up the monthly amounts for the "Regular Monthly Pay" section that we just went over. Write that total on the top of the worksheet in the "Total Monthly Income" box. And you're done with this part of the process.

Please be sure to finish all the calculations for master categories and income before you move on to the next lesson. If you are still in process getting information about your debts, it is OK to move forward while you do so. It will be good for you to proceed and will keep you motivated to get all the information, so you have a crystal-clear picture of your finances.

After you've let yourself relax for a day or so, I'll see you in the next lesson.

WORKSHEET #4 INCOME

Monthly Income Source	Amount Received Monthly
Paycheck	

TOTAL:

How to Calculate Your Paycheck for the Monthly Amount (See Lesson #22)

			(Five week months)
Paid Weekly	One paycheck x 4		One paycheck x 52 / 12
Type one paycheck amount	Monthly Amount		Monthly Amount
			(Counting the two extra checks)
Paid Bi-Weekly (every two weeks)	One paycheck x 2		One paycheck x 26 / 12
Type one paycheck amount	Monthly Amount		Monthly Amount
Paid Bi-Monthly (twice a month, such as on the 15th and 30th of the month)	One paycheck x 2		
Type one paycheck amount	Monthly Amount		

END OF INCOME WORKSHEET

• LESSON #23 •

Adding Up Your Master Categories and Income

IF YOU'RE USING THE EXCEL version of the workbook, and have completed the previous lesson, you don't have to do anything because the workbook automatically calculates these totals. You can move on to next lesson.

If you are using the PDF version of the workbook, you are going to look at worksheet #2. If you didn't finish this from the earlier lesson, you will add up all the subcategories under each master category and fill in the Master Category total. Those of you with debt already have a head start on this lesson as you've already transferred your total monthly debt to worksheet #2.

So, for instance, in the medical master category, add up the totals for prescription, doctor, dentist, etc. Write that number on each master category total line.

	Skip categories not relevant to you.	
MASTER Category	**SUBCATEGORY**	**Monthly Payment**
Medical	TDDoctor	$45
	TDDentist	$30
	TDPrescriptions	$100
	TDMedical Appliances	$1
Master Category Total	Supplements	$60
$237	Books on conditions	$1

After you are sure you have added up the subcategory totals for each master category, you are going to add up all the master category totals. So, for instance, you'll now add the medical master category to the grocery master category to the housing master category, etc.

When you get the total of all your master categories, write it down on worksheet #5, next to "Total Spending." In the print version of the book, this worksheet is located at the end of the next lesson.

WORKSHEET #5 FOUNDATIONAL NUMBER
Your Foundational Number is the difference between what you bring in and what you spend

TOTAL MONTHLY INCOME:
TOTAL SPENDING:

Now, go to worksheet #4 and be sure you have added up all your monthly income. (Remember, don't include sporadic income or windfalls.) Then, write that total number down on worksheet #5 next to "Total Monthly Income."

Fearless Budgeting Training Program

WORKSHEET #5 FOUNDATIONAL NUMBER
Your Foundational Number is the difference between what you bring in and what you spend

TOTAL MONTHLY INCOME:
TOTAL SPENDING:

This is a short lesson, but it was important to give yourself some space between all that work you did on your subcategories, debt, and income before you finish up with the simple task of totaling them up.

Remember that these are still just numbers on paper. They have no meaning yet. And we're very close to finishing up your spending plan foundation.

Hopefully, this part will be quick and easy, so I'll see you shortly in the next lesson.

• LESSON #24 •

Calculating Your Foundational Number

OK, HERE'S WHERE THE RUBBER meets the road. By this point, you're a seasoned warrior. Hopefully, numbers are no longer the terrifying monsters they were when you started. But this is the lesson that is a turning point. We are nearly at the end of the foundational spending plan training. What you do after this lesson is where you see your true strength, determination, and spirit.

I know you can do this. And before I give you the instructions, I'm going to make a couple of suggestions.

I strongly suggest doing this lesson with someone in your support network, and absolutely, positively, NOT a family member or partner. Please trust me on this. You need someone who understands, cares about you, and has no vested interest in, or who might make a judgment about, your spending. While you are definitely stronger than you were when you began this process, you are still most likely fragile and feeling a measure of shame, disappointment, or regret around your spending. So, far, this has all been a theoretical exercise. But in this lesson, it's going to get real.

So, let's get started. This is a short lesson. But it is the moment of truth. The moment where you see the reality. I believe that you have toughened up through this process and you will understand that this is just a pain point you have to move through like all the rest. This is a moment of hope because your willingness to face reality through the Fearless Budgeting training is the beginning of your new, healthier relationship with money.

If you are using the Excel workbook, your foundational number has been automatically calculated for you. If you are using the PDF version of the workbook, you will manually calculate your foundational number.

You will be using worksheet #5 (also at the end of this lesson). Now, you should have the total monthly income and total spending listed. If you're using the PDF version of the workbook, what I want you to do is to **subtract the total of your spending from your total monthly income and write**

that amount next to "Your Foundational Number" in the worksheet. I'd like you to pause and do the calculation and come right back to this lesson.

If you are using the Excel workbook, pause this recording, and go ahead and open it to worksheet #5. You will see your foundational number already filled in.

I'm glad you're back. Now, I want you to do the calming breath with me. Take a long, slow, deep breath in...

And slowly release it.

Pause.

If you're like most people, your foundational number is a negative number. But you did not faint. No monster came to grab you. Everything is just as it was before seeing that number.

Except for one very crucial thing. You have a clarity you lacked until now. You came through alive and stronger than you were before. And you now see the truth about your spending. This is a moment to feel entirely hopeful. There's no point in looking at a number on a piece of paper and thinking all is lost. It's not.

Now, you have a foundation and a framework. So, it's time to celebrate! And then, it's time to decorate your new "home" by transforming this foundation and structure into a spending plan. But before we go there, please reach out and talk to others about how you're feeling.

Fearless Budgeting Training Program

WORKSHEET #5 FOUNDATIONAL NUMBER
Your Foundational Number is the difference between what you bring in and what you spend

TOTAL MONTHLY INCOME: _____

TOTAL SPENDING: _____

YOUR FOUNDATIONAL NUMBER: _____

The objective is for your Foundational Number to be 0. In that case, you have successfully allocated all your income to categories.

If your foundational number is in the negative (red), then you will go back to sheet #2 and reduce the amounts in subcategories. **See Lessons #24 and #25 for instructions on how to adjust your spending plan.**

Copyright 2018 © Getting Out from Going Under Publishing FearlessBudgeting.wordpress.com

END OF WORKSHEET #5 FOUNDATIONAL NUMBER

SECTION IV:

TRANSFORMING THE FOUNDATION INTO A SPENDING PLAN

• LESSON #25 •

It's All About Choices

YOU NOW HAVE A COMPLETE spending plan foundation. There are just a few more steps before you have the first iteration of your working spending plan. I say the first iteration because it's going to take some time for you to live with the spending plan and use it to learn where you need to make changes. And this process goes on for a long time.

It's like buying a new pair of shoes. They may pinch a bit or feel stiff, but as you wear them, eventually they fit your foot like a glove and you can't imagine how you got along without them. And that's what's going to happen if you commit to working with your spending plan.

So, first, I'm going to tell you what happens next, and then, I'll give you some suggestions on how to accomplish it.

If you're incredibly fortunate, your foundational number is less than your income. If so, congratulations! For the 99.9 % of the rest of us, it's now time to begin making choices about how we spend our money. What you're going to do is work with this foundation to reduce the amount spent in your subcategories until your outflow equals your inflow.

I know this is the moment you've dreaded. I completely understand. But this is the moment to reaffirm your commitment and know that you are not alone. Thousands and thousands of people, including me, have been exactly where you are at this moment, facing this sobering truth. They kept moving forward, eventually getting to a place of balance in their spending plan. You can do this too.

The Two Types of Categories

Now, before we talk about how to proceed, I just want to go over the two types of categories you have in your spending plan. Essentially, they boil down to wants and needs. And when you are just starting out on this journey, and have to make hard decisions around your spending, it can be tough determining which is which.

Some of you know that because of how you get paid, you will be getting extra paychecks periodically or you may get a bonus or other sporadic income to augment your spending plan. That should give you some sense of calm. But even so, I'm still asking you to focus on matching your spending plan to the regular monthly income if you can.

There are obvious need categories, such as: housing, utilities, transportation, food, clothing, and medical. But wait, let's break that down a little further. Is it a need to have a new luxury vehicle instead of a used car? Is it essential to buy designer clothing? And this is where it becomes a learning process that is best done with the support of others to help you know the difference.

Yes, my theoretical questions may sound ridiculous, but I can tell you that I've certainly had my own share of wants that I insist are needs. **But I became willing to shift my thinking in order to live within my means.** I'll give you some examples later in the lesson.

Adjusting Your Spending Plan

So on to how to technically begin the process of adjusting your spending plan. First, if you are using the PDF version of the workbook, I strongly suggest that you now move to an electronic format to help you with the calculations because it may be challenging to keep track of where you've reduced and added when manually calculating numbers. Of course, you can still do this on paper, but I know that I make so many mistakes in calculating that there's no way I could do this on paper, myself. I also make mistakes typing numbers, so at the least, I do what I can to minimize problems.

You may want to start by downloading the Excel version of the workbook from the Foundational Course and typing in your information in worksheet #2A. While this is not a way to work with your spending plan ongoing, it may be a step toward feeling more comfortable using software.

For those who have been working with the Excel version of the workbook, you can feel free to continue adjusting your spending plan using worksheet #2A and then looking at worksheet #5 to see your updated foundational number.

Using the Excel version of the workbook is an excellent way to get your spending plan ready to actually begin using it. However, there will be a point at which you will need to shift from adjusting your foundation to working with a living, breathing spending plan, and you won't be able to do that in the Excel workbook.

Introduction to YNAB® (You Need a Budget)

There are many options for budgeting software around, and I'll be going over them in a later lesson, but my budgeting software preference is YNAB (You Need a Budget). The reason I recommend YNAB (and no, I don't work for YNAB) is that it's a simple virtual envelope system. It's as close as you can get to keeping track of your money by putting cash in envelopes, which is the cleanest, simplest method for compulsive spenders.

You'll get three months absolutely free to test out the software through my YNAB affiliate link. You don't even need to give them your billing information. Here is a shortened URL you can use to access it: tinyurl.com/fbynab (Link is in the resources handout as well.)

In the next course, "Working with Your Spending Plan," I will be using YNAB for screen shots and demonstrations. So, you may want to at least take advantage of the three free months to get familiar with the concepts I discuss and demonstrate.

Moving from the Fearless Budgeting Workbook to YNAB

It's really easy to make the move to YNAB from the workbook. All you need to do is to type the master and subcategories you created using the workbook into the YNAB "Budget" screen, along with the amounts you allocated to each category. YNAB's terminology is slightly different from Fearless Budgeting.

Fearless Budgeting Term	YNAB Term
Master Category	Category Group
Subcategory	Category

When you first create your new spending plan in YNAB, you'll notice that it contains their preconfigured category groups (master categories) and categories (subcategories). All you have to do is overwrite them with your own information. You can move, edit, add, and delete category groups and categories easily in YNAB.

SUSAN B.

Add New Categories and Groups in YNAB

The resources handout contains a link to a helpful document from YNAB describing how to add new category groups and categories.

Overwrite a Category Group and Subcategory in YNAB

Here is how to overwrite a category group and category:

1. Click on the name of the Category Group or Category to edit.

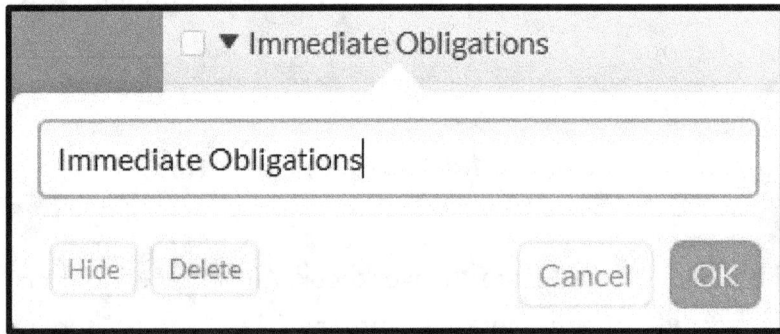

2. Type the new name for the master or subcategory.

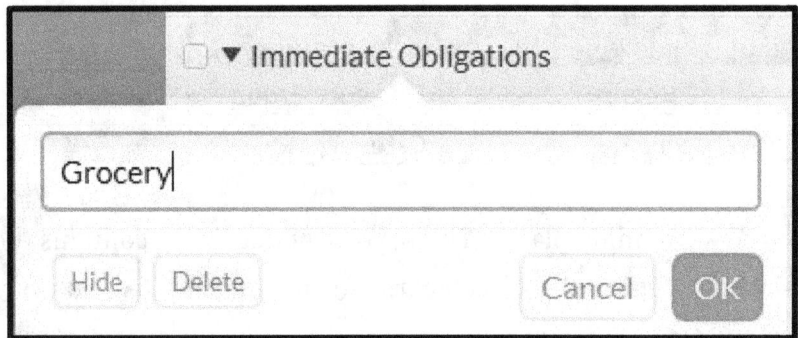

3. Click OK.

Move a Category Group or Category in YNAB

To move a category group or category:

1. Click on the name of the category and hold down the left mouse button.
2. Then, drag it to the new location.

You can easily move a category to a new category group and reorder groups and categories.

TRANSFERABLE SKILLS

No matter what budgeting solution you end up using, you will be able to translate the concepts I'm teaching you to meet the way your software works. And even if you end up using pen and paper, you still need to understand and implement the concepts and components crucial to an effective spending plan.

So, that addresses the technical solution.

Getting Help to Make Sober Choices

The more pressing issue is how on earth to figure out how to balance this spending plan foundation. Well, I definitely wouldn't do this alone. The problem is, if you're a true compulsive spender, you're not going to be able to figure this out alone. It's likely that you'll make extreme decisions you won't be able to live with or experience denial about categories you need to fund.

The thing is, you are most likely going to experience frustration and resistance, and stewing about it on your own is not going to move you into the light. You need help to see your choices differently. You need help to get right-minded about what types of spending are truly essential and what you can do without for now. It won't be forever. Once you bring your spending in balance, you will see that the way opens to enable you to satisfy more wants as well as to learn how to be happier with less. I can tell you this is true for me.

And here's where I'm putting in a big, big plug for Debtors Anonymous (DA), a free Twelve Step program which has a process in place for this very thing that has worked for thousands of people. So, I'm going to talk about the DA process just so you understand how this process works and you can translate it to make it work in your own life. I believe this process works best through the DA program, but if you can figure out another way to accomplish it, that's just fine.

The process is called a pressure relief group (or PRG). And, it's the stuff of miracles. Hard to think that anything to do with numbers could have any semblance of miracle in it. But it does.

So, two other recovering compulsive debtors help a third one to "relieve the pressure." (I call them debtors, but you don't have to be in debt to benefit from this program.) They aren't financial planners. They can't tell you how to invest your money. But they can share their experience, strength, and hope to help you sculpt a spending plan that will be balanced and work for you.

They can brainstorm with you to help you make choices around how much you allocate to categories or even how to bring in more income. And they can help you get willing to see the truth about things you think you can't live without. But nobody forces you to do anything.

The reason this is such an amazing thing is that you'll often have two people on your team who are quite different, maybe vastly different in career, income, and outlook on life. Yet, together with you, and yes, there is that Higher Power in attendance as well, but no need to think about that right now, solutions to impossible situations see the light of day.

In my own life, after I became disabled, I had Social Security Disability Insurance and private disability insurance. I was terrified of losing the private disability and was squeaking by as it was. For three years, I lived in terror that I wouldn't be able to make it financially without debting if that happened. And then, it happened. My worst fear. Over half my reduced income gone.

But with the help of my PRG team, I've been able to continue living within my means since that happened. And this miraculous process is offered absolutely free of charge. I only go to meetings on the telephone, never live because there are none near me. All the PRGs I give and get are by phone.

So, if for no other reason than to get the benefit of the help to make your spending plan work for you, I urge you to give Debtors Anonymous a chance. But I believe that if you do, you'll see rewards you can't even imagine today.

Alright, I'm off my soapbox now. So, you know my feelings about this. But if DA is just not an option for you, then, take the essence of what I've described and see if you can find one or, preferably, two people who can sit with you and help you sort through this. You probably can't do this in an hour, but over the course of three or four, you might be amazed at how much you accomplish.

Shifting Your Perceptions

When you are adjusting your spending plan foundation, it's important to shift your perception around this process. Notice that I didn't say you have to "cut" from categories. That's an inflammatory word that evokes deprivation. Yes, you *are* going to have to come to terms with the finite nature of money. While there may be an endless abundant supply in the universe, the fact is, you have a set amount of money. Debt isn't free money, so you need to make choices about how you spend the finite amount of money you do have in order to spend no more than you bring in. Working on bringing in more is another matter entirely.

For those who are underearning or in a dire financial situation, this process will be more challenging and take longer, there's no doubt about it. While you may not be able to adjust your spending so it doesn't exceed your income immediately, you can set your sights on that goal.

But in all cases, if you shift your language and your perception from deprivation and cutting to balance and choice, you begin to move into a new and sober relationship with your money. Yes, you may need to let go of some discretionary spending that you feel you can't live without ... for the time being. Or you may be able to continue funding these categories, just allocating less for now.

One of the most frequent distress cries I hear is about reducing spending on coffee out or restaurants. For some people, it's a lifestyle and the way they socialize. But often, they come to see that they spend so much more money than they imagined on coffee or eating out. And, when they realize how much of their income goes to these activities, if they are serious about doing this work, they become willing to change their lifestyle.

Maybe they choose to eat at home before they go out, and just have a salad or snack at the restaurant. Or they may eat out less often. Perhaps they decide to reduce the number of times they buy coffee when they go out.

It doesn't mean you can't hang out with friends at the coffee shop. It just means you don't have to spend money doing so. Everyone I've ever known who had these issues and made the choice to shift their perspective (and, consequently, their spending) was glad they did. It's not all or nothing. It's about balance.

I'll give you another example. I love buying books, but, I realized that too many times, I never even read them after buying them. Books were too often an impulse purchase for me. At this point, reading is tough with my visual issues, so I usually just skim anyway. But I still love books!

Now I use the library, which is a fantastic resource. I can have a book binge at the library without spending a penny! And 99% of the time, I realize I wouldn't have wanted to buy the book at all. So, my fear about not having enough money to buy books became a non-issue.

And I'll give you one more example, one that still pains me to talk about though it turned out to be for the best. I was paying for my son's college education, and then became disabled in his freshman year, which reduced my income. The hardest truth I had to swallow was that I could no longer afford to pay for his living expenses beginning with his sophomore year if I wanted to continue to live within my means in a balanced way. It took four people to help me grudgingly accept this, and the guilt I experienced was nearly unbearable. In the end, it turned out to be the best gift I ever gave my son, a life-changing opportunity for him to learn about financial responsibility, which he first bristled at, but ended up embracing. In fact, I wrote an article about this for a magazine called, "The Billfold." (You'll find the link in the resources handout.)

So, as you proceed to hone your spending plan, talk to others about where it makes sense to reduce your spending. Because you are now on this journey, I think a still, small voice inside will nudge you when you know you need to reduce the amount in a category but you're resistant . This voice will remind you that this is really fear of lack and your addict mind trying to sabotage you. You are going to be amazed at the inner strength you gain when you are willing to be honest with yourself as you go through this process.

Here is an exercise I want you to do every time you begin work on modifying your spending plan foundation:

1. Close your eyes.
2. Start by taking your calming breath as we've done so many times before.
3. And then, tell yourself that you are on your way to living in balance with your spending.
4. Then, tell yourself that you are going to make choices about where you allocate your money based on your intention to live in a balanced way within your means.
5. Say "thank you" out loud. That is acknowledgment that you appreciate and recognize the courage it takes for you to continue to do this work.

Please feel free to email me any time to ask questions or to let me know how you're doing. Don't forget you can also leave your questions in the student discussion forum.

• LESSON #26 •

Congratulations!

YOU HAVE NOW COMPLETED THE FEARLESS Budgeting "Foundational Course: Creating Your Spending Plan." You have come such a long way from where you began this journey. You now have the makings of a spending plan, one that is uniquely yours and that fits your life. I hope you recognize how much you have accomplished.

Now, *having* a spending plan and *using* a spending plan are two different things. It's great to have numbers written on a piece of paper or typed in a spreadsheet or even in a budgeting software program.

But now, you need to learn a simple and manageable way to work with your spending plan ongoing. And that's what I teach in the next course, which is called "Working with Your Spending Plan." As with the foundational course, the online version of the "Working with Your Spending Plan" course is absolutely free and contains all the training. So you can feel free to listen at any time.

You can certainly start the next Fearless Budgeting course while you're still working on transforming your foundation into a spending plan, because, as I've said, your spending plan is an evolving tool. It is never static and set in stone. So, right now, yes, you're making lots of adjustments to your plan. But there's no reason you can't begin to use it. Please don't let the perfect be the enemy of the good. The sooner you begin making your spending plan an integral part of your life, the sooner you can become more balanced in your spending.

But remember, a spending plan is an essential tool, but it's not a cure for compulsive spending. So, as I have repeated throughout this course, I urge you to find a recovery path and a network of support to help you heal this devastating addiction.

As I mentioned in the last lesson, I use, and recommend, YNAB as my preferred budgeting program. However, the concepts I teach will be applicable to any budgeting system, software program, or even if you use a spreadsheet or paper, pencil, and envelopes for tracking. Again, through my affiliate link, you can test YNAB out for three months absolutely FREE (no payment information required). So,

I strongly suggest you download it and use it along with the course, which will only take you a week or two to complete. That way, even if you don't stay with YNAB, you'll have real-world experience in putting the Fearless Budgeting concepts into practice. YBAB has great tutorials, an active support forum, and free live classes on the basics.

And don't forget to check out the "Getting Out from Going Under Daily Reader for Compulsive Debtors and Spenders" and the Five-Year Recovery Journal. The PDF version of the journal is free to download.

Would You Please Review this Course?

And if you have found this course helpful, I'd really appreciate a review. In the online course, just click the button that says, "Rate this course!" in the upper right-hand corner. If you are reading the print or e-book version, please consider leaving an Amazon review. Thanks so much for your support.

COURSE II

WORKING WITH YOUR SPENDING PLAN

SECTION I:

BEFORE YOU BEGIN

• LESSON #1 •

Welcome

WELCOME TO THE FEARLESS BUDGETING course - "Working with Your Spending Plan." If you don't have a spending plan yet, you will need to take the "Foundational Course: Creating a Spending Plan" so that you can bring a plan to work with. If you're here with your spending plan foundation, I'm assuming you already understand why it's crucial to have a spending plan. And because this course is geared to compulsive spenders, it's likely that you have struggled with spending in the past.

While this course won't cure your compulsive spending, if you are in some type of recovery program, it will be an invaluable adjunct to help you get the most out of using a spending plan, which is a crucial tool for any recovering compulsive spender.

While the foundational course walks you through the process of developing a spending plan foundation, in this course, we move from having a spending plan on paper to learning how to fully embrace the spending plan and use it in our daily life.

I'll take you step-by-step through this process, so that you are ready to begin working with your spending plan no matter how you intend to do so. While I do use a particular software package called YNAB for my screen shots and demonstrations, the concepts I'll be covering will be helpful no matter how you choose to work with your spending plan.

Whether you are new to this process or came to the course to get some help with your existing spending plan, I highly recommend that you take the time to go through each lesson in order as they build on each other, and even seasoned users may gain new insights through the process.

You will have access to all audios and lesson transcripts online plus you can email me any questions you might have or post a question in the student discussion forum. Please be sure to download the resources handout, which contains the links to any resources I mention in the lessons.

You can opt to order a downloadable version of the audios and transcript (with screen shots) for the Fearless Budgeting training program to listen and read offline. There is also a print and e-book edition of the entire training program, containing both courses, available.

I've also written a daily reader for compulsive spenders and debtors. You may find it to be helpful as you go through this process. Check out sample pages from the "Getting Out from Going Under Daily Reader for Compulsive Debtors and Spenders."

Finally, if you enjoy journaling, you may want to download the free PDF version of my Five-Year Recovery Journal. Again, see the resources document for all the links.

The time line for the "Working with Your Spending Plan" course is one to two weeks, depending on how quickly you move through it. This training course consists of four sections and 24 lessons.

If you have not yet signed up for email updates, I urge you to go to the do so if you are interested in additional support options. Just go to FearlessBudgeting.wordpress.com to sign up. For instance, through this mailing list you will get information on "open office hours" where you can call in on a free conference-call line to ask me questions, when this option becomes available.

In the next lesson, I'm going to talk about the different ways you can work with your spending plan and I'll give you more information about the budgeting software I recommend, and a link for you to test out this software for free for the next three months. Even if you don't end up sticking with it, you will be able to transfer what you've learned to any other budgeting solution you choose.

See you there.

• LESSON #2 •

Components of an Effective Spending Plan

TO BEGIN WITH, LET'S TALK about the components of an effective spending plan. Now, you've already got master and subcategories, and you've filled in amounts next to each, remembering that these amounts will most likely change over time and/or due to a change in circumstances.

In the next lesson, I'm going to talk about the different options for maintaining and working with your spending plan. But you need to understand all the pieces that are required to make this process work well in a coordinated way.

Tracking Your Spending

You need to have a way to track your spending. So, that means that you have to be able to write or type somewhere what you spent and what you spent it on. A check register can be an effective way to track spending. So, can a notebook, carried with you. Or, keeping your receipts and writing down what you spent when you get home. You'll also want to be able to track your debts and credit card spending (hopefully, none) and how much is left to pay off your debts, accounting for interest.

Organizing Your Spending

You need a way to organize and total your daily spending by categories. This way you can see how much you spent overall AND how much is left in that category to spend. Just writing down your individual transactions won't tell you much. So, you need an easy way to know if you are overspending ...

preferably, before you spend it. This means you have to develop the habit of looking at your spending plan categories before making purchases.

Knowing Your Available Category Funds

You also need an easy way to know how much you have available to spend in your categories before you spend money. Otherwise, well, otherwise, chaos will ensue. It's a domino effect. If you overspend in one category, it has to come from somewhere. And then, when you want to spend from that somewhere and don't have enough, well, then, there goes another somewhere. And eventually, the entire structure comes crashing down.

The Magical Effect of Accumulating Money in Your Categories

If you want a functional spending plan, then you must have a way to accrue in categories. Accrue is another word for accumulate. I can't stand the word save because, just hearing it makes me want to spend!

One reason I'm in love with my spending plan is that I have enough categories that I don't obsess over each individual category as it automatically accrues. What I mean is that I allocate a certain amount from my income to each subcategory, and, that same amount gets added to that subcategory month after month. There are categories that I spend from monthly, others, quarterly, and some, like my dog license or Amazon Prime membership, annually.

It's psychological, but this has made it easier for me to allow money to increase for specific items. I go into this topic in depth in the Foundational Spending Plan course. But, essentially, what this means is that I divide all my bills by the number of months until they are due and then allocate that amount monthly. That way, I don't have to scramble to find the total due at the last minute.

The software program I use for my spending plan automatically adds what's left over in every subcategory at the end of the month to the amount I've allocated for the next month. Here's an example. I allocated $500 for groceries this month, and only spent $475, which means I'll start next month with the $500 I allocate each month PLUS the $25 that was left over from last month, for a total of $525 available to spend.

Too many people don't think about this, but it's really important. A number of years ago, I wanted to get a passport. The price at the time was $120, which seemed an impossible amount for me to accumulate. As a compulsive spender, I want what I want NOW. I don't want to wait for it. But because I live by my spending plan (and have learned to appreciate delayed gratification), I created a subcategory for the passport and allocated $10 to it each month. I didn't think about it, it was automatic. A year later, there was the $120 in that category! Yes, it was a year later, but I made the amount something that that felt reasonable to me, that I wouldn't miss too badly each month, and didn't obsess over it.

The Danger of Rounding

You must account for your cash in your spending plan and you need to track the pennies and not round up. I speak about this in the foundational course, but it bears repeating. This is a sore spot with many compulsive spenders. The thing is, we want to be clear about our money. And, like it or not, pennies, dimes, nickels, and quarters do make up dollars.

Think about it. Would you like it if the bank eliminated the pennies? So, if you get a check for $297.45, they only give you $297. Or what if a store rounded up? So, for instance, if a pair of shoes costs $89.58, they didn't want to deal with change and charged you $90. Would you like that?

Over time, that change you receive and spend makes a big difference. And getting clear with your spending means getting clear with all your spending. When you are actually using the spending plan, you'll understand that what your spending plan says is available must match what the bank shows as available (which I'll talk about next) in order for your spending plan to be useful. Please trust me that rounding up or down is going to eventually lead to vagueness, which is dangerous for a compulsive spender.

And Finally, the Secret Sauce

Finally, and this is the key to having an effective spending plan, you must be able to reconcile your spending plan with your bank accounts and your cash. Reconcile means that the amount that your spending plan says you have available when all the money that's left in each category is totaled up is equal to the amount that the bank (or your wallet in the case of cash) shows is available.

This is a complex topic for many people, and I'm going to do a whole lesson and a video to walk you through this process. I have a simple, easy way for you to do this. The fact is, if you can't trust the accuracy of your spending plan, well, it's pretty much useless. Numbers are precise. There are easy ways to streamline this process that I'll teach you so you always know that your accounts are reconciled.

Now, here are some thoughts on other functionality that is not essential, but can make your life a lot easier:

SUSAN B.

Track All Your Accounts and Gift Cards

Tracking savings and other accounts, like gift cards, is very helpful. While transactions in these categories don't necessarily affect your spending plan, wouldn't it be helpful to have clarity around all your money? I don't know about you, but, too often in the past, I would totally lose track of gift cards and never get the benefit intended from them. So, having a way to keep track of every money avenue in my life is important to me.

One Spending Plan to Track All Your Accounts

If you have multiple checking accounts, it's very helpful to have a way to automatically deduct spending in your categories from all your accounts at once, rather than having a separate spending plan for each checking account.

Easy Tax Reporting

This a component that I find necessary but may not be as important to you. It's generating reports for taxes. Having an easy way to group spending or income information to get a grand total of the past quarter or past year is an enormous time saver at tax time and can greatly reduce the stress headaches that usually accompany doing our taxes. If you're using an accountant, organizing your taxes could result in reduced costs.

So, that's pretty much it. Let me know if there's a feature or function that I missed that's important to you.

I'll see you in the next lesson.

• LESSON #3 •

Options for Working with Your Spending Plan

THERE ARE MANY OPTIONS FOR working with a spending plan. I'm going to outline each type and then give you my recommendation.

The Envelope Method

Some compulsive spenders in recovery do not trust themselves with checks and/or debit cards. Since I believe that credit cards are crack to a compulsive spender, I'm not even factoring them in at this point. I'll talk a lot more about debt in the bonus section, and I will have a lesson on how to handle credit card payments later.

Some compulsive spenders only use cash for spending, and that feels safer for them. If necessary, they'll go to the bank and get a bank check or money order when needed. Or they may have some automatic debits set up in their checking account.

But for the most part, these people choose to work with a series of envelopes with the name of a category on each, and the money allocated to that category for the month inside the envelope. When the money is gone, that is the end of spending in that category unless they take money from another envelope. I'll have a lesson on the concept of moving money between categories later.

At the beginning of the month, they write on the envelope the amount of money they put in the envelope. If there was money left over the previous month, they add that to the total. Every time they remove money from the envelope, they write what they spent it on and subtract it from the running total on the envelope.

This method does meet all the requirements for an effective spending plan. It's a simple, straightforward system and works beautifully for some people. Bank reconciliation is simple if all your spending is cash or money order or bank check. For most people, though, at least some of their spending is through a debit card or check, so you still need a method to account for, and reconcile, that portion of your spending with your bank account.

Unfortunately, for me, I lose cash all the time. I try to keep as little cash around as possible because I can't seem to keep track of it. And I wouldn't be comfortable keeping a lot of cash on hand. So, this wouldn't be a good option for me, but for those who prefer living on a cash basis for some or all of their spending, it's a great idea because it's pretty well free, except for a few envelopes and a pen.

A Spreadsheet

Some people use a spreadsheet to track their spending. But if you don't know how to create spreadsheet calculations, it can be challenging to make it truly functional. For instance, you need a way to accumulate in categories from month to month and year to year. However, you can buy spreadsheets that are already set up with all the formulas you need.

Budgeting Software

Budgeting software is my preferred method because it takes so much labor-intensive calculating and keeping numbers straight out of my hands. A good program does all the following automatically:

- Associates each transaction with a category
- Accumulates month by month in your categories
- Makes reconciling easy
- Has reporting capabilities, and
- Syncs across all devices.

There are dozens of budgeting software options like Mint, Every Dollar, and Quicken. I've tested a few, including these. But I keep coming back to YNAB, which is short for You Need a Budget, because I've not found any other solution that comes close to their virtual envelope system. I also think it's the best budgeting software I've found for compulsive spenders to organize, track, and accrue in categories. You can try YNAB for free for three months if you use my affiliate link (no payment information required). The shortened URL is tinyurl.com/fbynab.

There are just certain elements that we need that I've found lacking or more difficult to use with other options. For instance, YNAB makes moving money between categories really simple, which is not the case with EveryDollar. Another thing I love about YNAB is the natural way you allocate money to categories in real time, just like with envelopes, rather than having to set up a distinct budget as a separate entity, which you have to do in Mint, for instance.

Please Don't Link Your Bank Accounts to Your Budgeting Software

With Mint, you HAVE to link your online bank accounts with the software. OH NO! That is something I *definitely* don't want you to do. YNAB gives you that option, but I implore you not to use it. Aside from any concerns we all have about security, compulsive spenders need as much clarity as possible.

When transactions automatically download, there is an enormous risk of error and vagueness. For example, you may not recognize payee information or you may not want the category that was selected by the software. So, now you have to fix the transaction anyway. Or, you may not realize that a fraudulent transaction had occurred, or there has been a bank error, because you just don't review each transaction as it comes in because you just assume it's correct.

By manually entering each transaction into YNAB (which is really simple because it looks just like a check register), you make it much more likely that you will catch a bank error, or even a fraudulent transaction, when you reconcile. If you just import the transactions from the bank and don't review each one, then reconciling with your account is pointless because both will contain the same error.

Look, most people only make a few transactions a day, so typing them in keeps you crystal clear about your spending and just takes a minute or two. The more hands-on you are with your budget, the easier it is to work with and the more you can rely on it.

More about Why I Recommend YNAB

YNAB is not free and is not the cheapest option out there. And, yes, I've looked elsewhere to see if anything else will work me and for those I train. But so far, while some options come close, no other software has all the options compulsive spenders need.

My recommendation is that you at least try out YNAB for the duration of this course (remember, you have three whole months to test if out). Even if you don't end up buying it, you will really understand what to look for when deciding on a method to track your spending ongoing.

The other positive feature of YNAB is their extensive training. They have 20-minute live classes where you can ask questions in real time as well as lots of written documentation for basic functionality. They also have a vibrant user forum where people will be happy to help you.

While I have created a complete walk-through video of how I use YNAB, please understand that I am not going to recreate, in this course, what they've already done so well, which is how to use the core YNAB functionality, such as how to create and move categories, for instance. YNAB has great tutorials, active support forum, and free live classes on the basics. And, of course, you can always email me with questions as well or post your question in the student discussion forum.

Since you can complete the course well within the framework of the free three-month trial period, once the course is over, if you don't want to continue with YNAB, just cancel the account, and take the concepts you've learned and transfer them to whatever system you end up using.

Please be sure to sign up for the Fearless Budgeting email updates. If there does seems to be a need for me to provide additional training, I'll announce it through the mailing list when available.

Remember all links to resources I mention are contained in the resources handout.

SECTION II:

HOW WILL YOU TRACK YOUR SPENDING?

• LESSON #4 •

How do You Get Paid?

A DECISION YOU NEED TO make is what time frame you will use to track your spending. For most people, tracking by the month is best. Even if you get paid weekly or sporadically, there is no reason you can't track your expenses monthly. And certainly, if you are paid twice a month (also called semi-monthly, or every two weeks (also called bi-weekly), monthly tracking will work for you.

Admittedly, there are challenges around monthly tracking for those who get paid weekly. I will talk more about handling weekly income in a later lesson.

For those who make sporadic income, I still recommend tracking your spending by the month. Generally, I advise looking at the total income of the past year, for instance, found on your tax return, and then divide by 12 to get an average amount monthly.

The net income for employees is the actual check amount after any taxes, insurance, retirement plan contributions, etc. That's the amount you have available to spend. For those who make sporadic income, in general, you receive a gross paycheck, which is the amount before any taxes or other deductions are taken out.

For the first year, while you are getting up and running, here is what I recommend you do:

- If you are paid monthly, that's the total you will use for your spending plan.
- If you are paid twice a month, you will use the total of two checks for your spending plan.

Here is my recommendation for more complex situations:

- If you are paid weekly, you will get four paychecks most months, but you will receive five paychecks a few months of the year. If at all possible, I would base the spending plan monthly total on four net paychecks. Then, when you get the additional checks, you will allocate the money.

If you don't do it this way, you will definitely have a cash flow problem when you first begin, unless you have savings to cover it. I will explain this in detail when I get to the lesson on living in the next month.

- For those who get paid every two weeks (bi-weekly), you receive 26 paychecks a year. Again, I would base the spending plan on the total net income from two checks. Twice a year, you will receive an additional check.
- For both weekly and bi-weekly pay, the months in which these extra paychecks occur change based on the year and day of the month you are paid. When you receive the extra checks, you can then decide how to allocate the money.

What I Don't Recommend

I don't recommend including bonuses, royalties, item sales, or one-off fluctuating payments, like interest or dividends in figuring out the monthly amount of money you will base your spending plan on (even though you may receive them monthly). It's really best to keep the spending plan income total as consistent as possible.

And, then, when you get extra income, whether from these types of payments or extra paychecks, etc., you will be able to use the money to further fund your categories or for special items. I don't know about you, but many times, I counted on receiving a payment and it was delayed, or I anticipated selling a lot of product, but the actual monthly sales were far less than I'd hoped for. What's important to keep in mind is that you don't want to spend money before you receive it, or you could incur overdraft fees.

So, if possible, think of these variable income sources as extra money that you will account for when you receive it. Again, when you commit to living by a spending plan, you commit to spending based on money you have in hand, not in anticipation of what you will receive.

• LESSON #5 •

Living in the Next Month

THIS IS A KEY TOPIC for anyone who lives by a spending plan, but particularly for compulsive spenders. I used to live hand-to-mouth. That means, I barely scraped by until the next paycheck arrived. I think most of us live like that.

I've seen how challenging this can be for those paid weekly, because, for example, you may allocate $650 for groceries for the month, but only have a fraction of that available in the first week of the month. Or if you need to pay a bill in week one, you may have to account for that in the last week of the previous month if you won't get the current month's first week check in time.

Having a spending plan can relieve a lot of those issues just by the fact that you think through your spending for the month ahead of time.

However, there is really only one way to completely alleviate this problem, and that's living in the next month. And while it is most likely something you cannot yet do, I want you to know what to do and how to do it because it will change your life, and you can, at the least, start thinking about it right now.

What is Living in the Next Month?

Here's what living in the next month means: whatever I get paid in January, gets spent in February. What this means is that on February 1, I have an entire month's worth of income to allocate. So, I can buy the groceries I need and pay the bills that are due without the anxiety of waiting for the next paycheck before doing so ... or kiting checks and holding your breath hoping the money comes in before the check is cashed.

It's an incredible feeling to know your spending plan is fully funded on the first day of each month. But this is where I want you to begin to understand why you need to stop looking at the money in your bank account when you think about spending, but instead, look at your categories. Because if you follow this plan and eventually live in the next month, you will start to see a lot more money in your checking account. You'll understand what I mean in a moment.

How Do I Start Living in the Next Month?

So, how do you start this if you live paycheck to paycheck? Slowly, I suspect. Here's what I did. I stopped debting and compulsively spending in April of 2009. From that time, I lived by a spending plan, hand-to-mouth, paycheck to paycheck. Always really struggling to make it the few days before the next paycheck arrived.

In November of 2009, I learned about this concept of living in the next month when I began using YNAB. I think they called it the buffer then, and now, they call it aging money. But to me, it's just living in the next month.

By November, I had been able to accumulate money in a couple of savings categories. I had just enough to equal one month's worth of paychecks. I was terrified, just as I was when I cut up my credit cards and closed the accounts six months earlier. What would happen if I needed this money? But I had already seen the miraculous happen — because I had stopped compulsive spending, for one thing, and none of the crises I imagined had occurred when I canceled all those credit cards, for another.

So, I just steeled myself, believing that a Power greater than me would help me if I was just willing, and I moved the money from savings to income.

The first of the next month, I was jubilant when I saw that I could breathe easy and not worry about having enough food before my next paycheck. Now, that's not to say that I had abundantly filled categories, so there was no pressure. Heck no! That's a different issue entirely. But the spending plan as I had developed it was ready for me to use on day one of the month. And I've never gone back to living paycheck to paycheck since then.

Now, I've seen people make the mistake of thinking this buffer is free money to spend or to use in a non-emergency, emergency. And so these people never reap the rewards of living in the next month because they don't give this magical process time to work. They just go back to living paycheck to paycheck and feeling miserable.

It's a rubber meets the road place, where you need to have the emotional support (found in recovery programs) to help you learn to tolerate having money in the bank without feeling compelled to spend it all.

Can I Start Small?

So, what are you to do if you are living on the edge and don't have the resources to fund an entire day, much less a month, of your spending plan? In that case, I suggest that you create a savings subcategory called "Buffer" and even if you put a penny in that category each month, it has started a domino effect. If you are committed to this process, and diligent at living within your means and by your spending plan, little by little, you will find that you can accumulate more and more in the buffer until eventually, you have succeeded in accumulating one month's worth of income. It doesn't matter how long it takes to get there. It matters that you begin the journey.

If you are still confused about this concept, please email me or post a question in the student discussion forum.

Budgeting Software Tip When You Live Paycheck to Paycheck

To effectively use budgeting software, you must allocate only as much money as you have available to spend. Therefore, if you are paid weekly, bi-weekly, or semi-monthly, you will have a cashflow issue. The easiest way to manage this in your budgeting software is to track how much money is allocated to each category monthly, but only allocate a portion of that with each paycheck.

On the next page, you'll see an example using YNAB.

	JUN 2018 ▼			$0.00	+$1,000.00 Funds for Jun
	Enter a note...			To be Budgeted	-$0.00 Overspent in May
					-$1,000.00 Budgeted in Jun
					-$0.00 Budgeted in Future

⊕ Category Group ⤺ Undo ⤼ Redo

CATEGORY	BUDGETED	ACTIVITY	AVAILABLE
▼ Immediate Obligations	$1,000.00	$0.00	$1,000.00
Rent/Mortgage $575 due 1st	$575.00	$0.00	$575.00
Electric 75 due 17th	$5.00	$0.00	$5.00
Water $20 due 9th	$20.00	$0.00	$20.00
Internet $50 due 1st	$50.00	$0.00	$50.00
Groceries $875	$200.00	$0.00	$200.00
Gas 200	$125.00	$0.00	$125.00
Clothing $80	$0.00	$0.00	$0.00
Medical $125	$25.00	$0.00	$25.00

In this example, I get paid twice a month. Each paycheck is $1,000. Notice the following:

1. The first paycheck was received for $1,000. (See upper right corner of screen shot "+$1,000.00 Funds for Jun."
2. Next to each subcategory name, the total amount to be allocated for the month is listed, along with the due date, if applicable. For example:
    a. Rent/Mortgage is $575/month and it's due on the 1st of the month.
    b. Grocery spending for the month is funded at $875.
3. Now, you can only allocate as much money to categories as you have available if you want to live within your means. Therefore, any bills due before the next paycheck must be fully funded, such as the Rent/Mortgage.
4. But since you don't have enough to fully fund *all* your categories, you must make decisions as to how much to fund in each. For instance:
    a. You need groceries, but you still have plenty of food from the end of the last month. So you only allocated $200 of the $875 that will fund this category over the course of the month.
    b. You need to do more driving during the first half of the month, so you allocate more than half to gas.

c. Since the electric bill isn't due until after the next paycheck, that category is partially funded at $5 of the total due of $75. That will mean less to be funded with the next paycheck.

d. Clothing isn't funded at all, so no spending in that category until it's funded with the next check.

e. $25 is put into Medical just in case.

Now, the second paycheck comes in on the 15th. Here is how the spending plan might look before funding the additional money:

JUN 2018 — $1,000.00 To be Budgeted

+$2,000.00 Funds for Jun
-$0.00 Overspent in May
-$1,000.00 Budgeted in Jun
-$0.00 Budgeted in Future

CATEGORY	BUDGETED	ACTIVITY	AVAILABLE
▼ Immediate Obligations	$1,000.00	-$810.20	$189.80
Rent/Mortgage $575 due 1st	$575.00	-$575.00	$0.00
Electric 75 due 17th	$5.00	$0.00	$5.00
Water $20 due 9th	$20.00	$0.00	$20.00
Internet $50 due 1st	$50.00	$0.00	$50.00
Groceries $875	$200.00	-$119.45	$80.55
Gas 200	$125.00	-$115.75	$9.25
Clothing $80	$0.00	$0.00	$0.00
Medical $125	$25.00	$0.00	$25.00

1. Notice that there is now $1,000 available to be budgeted (top of screen).
2. The rent was paid and there was spending in Groceries and Gas.

So now, we can fully fund the rest of the categories with the second paycheck of $1,000.

(The example continues on the next page.)

	JUN 2018		$0.00 To be Budgeted	+$2,000.00 Funds for Jun -$0.00 Overspent in May -$2,000.00 Budgeted in Jun -$0.00 Budgeted in Future

CATEGORY	BUDGETED	ACTIVITY	AVAILABLE
▼ Immediate Obligations	$2,000.00	-$810.20	$1,189.80
Rent/Mortgage $575 due 1st	$575.00	-$575.00	$0.00
Electric 75 due 17th	$75.00	$0.00	$75.00
Water $20 due 9th	$20.00	$0.00	$20.00
Internet $50 due 1st	$50.00	$0.00	$50.00
Groceries $875	$875.00	-$119.45	$755.55
Gas 200	$200.00	-$115.75	$84.25
Clothing $80	$80.00	$0.00	$80.00
Medical $125	$125.00	$0.00	$125.00

Since I only receive two paychecks a month in this example, I just overwrote the budgeted amounts next to each subcategory with the full monthly amount listed in the category name. If you're paid weekly, then you'll continue just adding a portion each week to make it work out (or fully fund the entire amount of a bill that's due). I'll talk more about that in the next lesson.

Using your budgeting software in this manner will be challenging at first, but it will really help you live within your means as you learn to make choices. For instance, if you feel an urge to go out to eat two days before your next paycheck, and there is only $10 left in Groceries (in this example we'll pretend Groceries includes restaurants as well), you can make a decision to eat at home instead. In two days, you'll be able to eat out again. This will help you strengthen the muscle of delayed gratification, a topic I discuss in depth in lessons #9 and #19.

If you are still confused about this concept, please email me or post a question in the student discussion forum.

• LESSON #6 •

If You are Paid Weekly

THIS LESSON IS JUST FOR those who are paid weekly. Now, hopefully, you've already listened to the previous lesson about living in the next month. That's your goal. If you do this, you will not have any cash flow complexity in your spending plan. You'll have a fully funded spending plan on the first day of the month.

However, until then, let's talk about how to track your money most easily. As I said in an earlier lesson, I suggest you track your spending monthly and base your monthly spending plan on four weeks of net pay. Again, the net is the money you actually receive to spend. I realize that you will be getting a fifth paycheck periodically, but my recommendation is to account for the normal monthly paycheck amount when figuring out your spending plan. Otherwise, you may run into a cash flow issue before you've hit a month where you receive a fifth check.

If you used the Excel version of the Fearless Budgeting workbook, you already have monthly *and* weekly amounts listed in worksheet #2A. If you used the PDF version, you may have already done this work manually.

However, I've created an additional Excel worksheet you can download to help you out even further. (Link is in the resources handout and in this online lesson.) So, I'd like you to pause the lesson now, download it, and open it so that you can look at it as I explain how to use it.

OK, let's talk about this worksheet. Like the other workbook, you can type in the light pink areas. But please don't do anything until I've gone over this because there are some calculations that you will need to overwrite and I want you to understand how, and why, to do it before you begin.

1. So, the first thing you will do is to type in the amount of one paycheck underneath the instruction to type in the amount for one paycheck (located in cell A7).

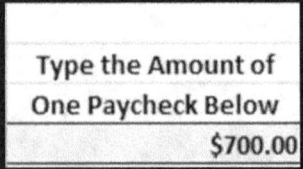

2. Then, you will type the first master category name in column A. For instance, Household.
3. Now, type in all the subcategories for that master category in column B, such as rent, electric, and cable.
4. On the line following the last subcategory for the master category (Household, in the example below), type the next master category in column A, such as Vehicle.
5. Then, in column B type in all the subcategories for that master category, such as car payment and gas. It should look something like this:

Master Categories	Subcategories
Household	Rent
	Electric
	Cable
Vehicle	Car payment
	Gas

6. After you've listed all your master and subcategories, enter all the monthly amounts you're allocating for each subcategory. For example:

Master Categories	Subcategories	Monthly Amount (for subcategories only)
Household	Rent	$500.00
	Electric	$75.00
	Cable	$50.00
Vehicle	Car payment	$350.00
	Gas	$75.00

7. As you fill in the monthly amounts, you can periodically check the Income-Expenses, located directly above the monthly amounts in cell C6. You will see how much is left of your income to allocate. In this example:
   - The single paycheck amount is $700.
   - The monthly amount is $2,800 ($700 x 4).
   - Right now, the amount entered into the expenses totals $1,050.
   - So, you can see there is still $1,750 left to allocate after you subtract the expenses from the income.

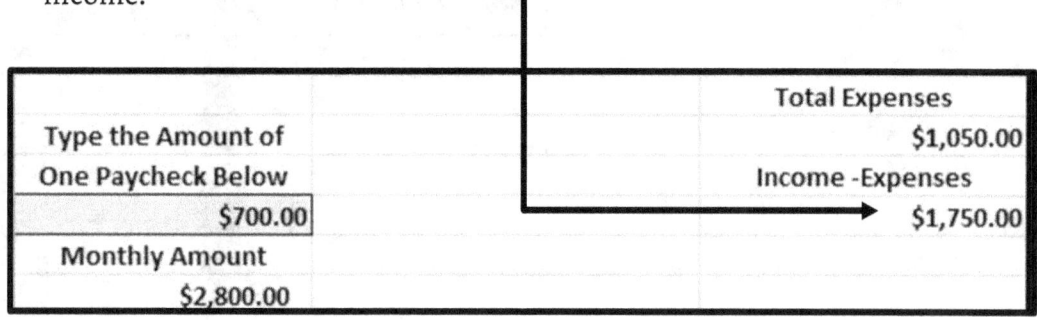

The key is for Income - Expenses to be 0 after you've filled in all your subcategories. That means that your expenses don't exceed your income and you've allocated every penny to a category.

How Bills Need to Be Funded

Once you've finished filling in the monthly amount for each subcategory and adjusted it so that Income - Expenses = 0, it's time to look at the weekly numbers. Just ignore the "Week Five" column for now. We're going to start with "Week One." (See screenshot on next page.)

Excel has automatically calculated 1/4 of the monthly amount in each weekly column, which means that categories won't be fully funded until you reach Week Four. That's a problem because some bills are due sooner. And you have to account for that. **So, before you even begin working on this spreadsheet, you need to know when all your bills are due so you can adjust this worksheet.**

Let's take an example. For instance, Rent is $500, but there is a problem! You need to pay your rent the first week of the month! Now, once you are able to fully or even partially, live in the next month, this will not be a problem. In that case, you may be able to start allocating the rent money in the previous month. But for now, let's just walk through this example as if you needed to use the Week One paycheck to fund the rent.

In the screenshot, you see that $125 is allocated to rent in Week One. That's 1/4 of the $500 total. Well, how will you pay the rent? What you'll need to do is to increase the Rent to $500 in Week One and then, you'd have to reduce the amount in other subcategories in Week One to make up the difference, which, in this case is $375. Here is what the worksheet looks like right now for "Week One:"

Master Categories	Subcategories	Monthly Amount (for subcategories only)	Week One
Household	Rent	$500.00	$125.00
	Electric	$75.00	$18.75
	Cable	$50.00	$12.50
Vehicle	Car payment	$350.00	$87.50
	Gas	$75.00	$18.75
Grocery	Food	$600.00	$150.00
	Restaurant	$250.00	$62.50
	House supplies	$63.01	$15.75
Insurance	Car insurance	$125.00	$31.25
	Renter's insurance	$95.00	$23.75
Entertainment	HBO	$11.99	$3.00
	Books	$25.00	$6.25
Medical	Health insurance	$450.00	$112.50
	Doctor visits	$40.00	$10.00
	Dentist	$30.00	$7.50
Wardrobe	Clothing	$40.00	$10.00
	Accessories	$20.00	$5.00

It's clear that if I change Rent from $125 to $500, I'll need to reduce the amount in lots of categories to make up for the shortfall, which is going to leave me strapped for cash in a lot of areas. But if you persist, you will eventually be able to fund more smoothly.

Making Up for Shortfalls

For instance, in Week Two, you may choose to put a little bit of money toward the next month's rent, which will offset the amount you'll need to reduce in week one of the next month. You will also be able to increase in areas that were reduced in Week One. But again, if any bills are due in Week Two, then you need to ensure that you fully fund those categories, which may mean reducing in others again. But keep at it because you will eventually make it work just as others have done before you.

Naturally, through this process, you will be overwriting the calculations I created in Excel in one or more categories. That is fine, and I expect you to do that. **But keep checking the Income-Expenses for the week you are adjusting to be sure you don't exceed the weekly income.** If you do, then you simply need to subtract the overage from one or more subcategories. Again, Income - Expenses must be zero.

Total Expenses	
	$775.00
Income - Expenses	
	($75.00)
Week One	
	$87.50
	$62.50
	$250.00
	$150.00
	$225.00

Now, if you accidentally overwrite a calculation, just copy the calculation from any other cell **in the same column** and paste it into the cell where you want the calculation to appear. In Windows:

1. Go to the cell to copy and press the CTRL key on your keyboard and the letter "c" to copy the formula.
2. Click in the cell where you want to paste the formula
3. Press the CTRL key on your keyboard and the letter "v" to paste it.
4. Then, press Enter.

I understand that this may sound complicated. But it will get easier as you work with it. If you do this process for all four weeks in the worksheet, then you will be able to reference it as you work with your budgeting software. So, for instance, if you use YNAB, you will be able to quickly and easily enter the amounts from each week accurately by just using this worksheet as your guide.

I did put in the fifth week just in case you wanted to figure out where to allocate the money when it comes in.

***

Next, be sure to go back and read the last section in the previous lesson (#5, Living in the Next Month) called "Budgeting Software Tip When You Live Paycheck to Paycheck." Follow the instructions to make your weekly allocations much more manageable.

***

If you need more help with this, please email me or post your question in the student discussion forum. This may be a good topic for the "open office hours" I'm contemplating where I can answer your questions in real time. When you write, let me know if you'd be interested.

• LESSON #7 •

More on Periodic Bills

IN THE FOUNDATIONAL COURSE, I went over how to figure out the monthly amount to allocate for bills that are not paid monthly. So, if a bill is due once a year, you simply divide it by 12 and the result is the amount you allocate each month. Or if, say, the car insurance is due every six months, you divide the total you pay by six. That's pretty straightforward.

But, before I go into more depth on this topic, I want to review what I went over in the Foundational course about bills that you pay periodically, such as those you pay quarterly (due four times a year) or at some other interval. For all of these types of bills, I suggest that you divide them up so that you accumulate for them monthly. For instance, I pay my $15 dog license annually. So, $15/12 months = $1.25. That's how much I need to accumulate monthly to be able to pay my dog license each year when it's due. It should be clear that allocating $1.25/month toward my dog license is a lot more doable than scrambling to find $15 when the license is due.

But I know that a lot of people get really upset at my suggestion, even angry, especially when it comes to such a small amount. They say that the bill isn't due for a year, and they need to use their money for other things now. But, see, this is exactly the attitude that needs to change if you want to learn to live within your means.

Why You Should Allocate All Your Bills Monthly

Think about it. You'll have to find that money somewhere at some point, and what if that $15-dollar dog license is due when you also have your annual $1,200 property tax bill due, along with your semi-annual (that means twice a year) $450 car insurance bill. If you accrue the funds for all these bills monthly, each one is a non-issue when it's due.

Think about how much you scramble to pay these types of bills now. In fact, you may have lost your car insurance because you couldn't scrape together $450 at the last minute. Or you might have been close to a lien on your house if you didn't have the $1,200 for the property tax bill. But if you took the time to divide each one of these periodic bills by the number of months before you need to pay them, and add up those monthly amounts, you'll see that it's a far more manageable number you need to accrue monthly, than the panicked impossible-to-find amount for each individual bill when it's due because you just pretended the due date was never coming. And now, I'm going to explain exactly how to do this.

Figuring Out the Monthly Total

Let's add up the totals for all three bills we've just discussed and then figure out the total we'd need to accumulate monthly to pay them.

- The property tax bill is $1,200.
- The dog license is $15.
- And the car insurance is $450.

That's $1,665.

So, let me break that down.

- The $1,200 tax bill divided by 12 months is $100/month.
- The dog license of $15/month divided by 12 is $1.25.
- And the car insurance of $450 divided by six is $75.

This means that the total you'd be allocating toward all three expenses $176.25/month.

Can you really, seriously say you'd rather go through the angst of finding the total of each of these bills at the last minute or be willing to get used to a fraction of that amount automatically socked away in its respective category month after month?

Look, there's always going to be an issue that can threaten to derail your best intentions. But if you are committed to finding peace of mind around your spending and live by your spending plan, and especially if you're a compulsive spender, you absolutely need to consider putting this suggestion into practice.

The Elephant in the Room

There is one more aspect to paying periodic bills that I need to explain to you. And if you need to take a pause before I continue, because I know I'm really in the weeds with these number right now, please pause this lesson and take a calming breath.

OK, are you ready to keep going? Good. When you first begin working with your spending plan, the due dates for periodic bills will be messy. By that, I mean that a bill may be due sooner than the normal time frame. So, let's take the dog license.

- It's due once a year in April.
- But if I start my spending plan in January, then it won't work to divide the $15 by 12 months, because the bill is due in four months **just this first time**.

To be safe, I suggest that you divide the $15 bill by three months. That means:

- I'll allocate $5 in January,
- $5 in February,
- And $5 in March.
- Then, I've got the money to pay the bill before it's due.

Beginning in April, I can allocate $1.25 to that category each month.

Facing Facts without Giving Up

Let's take another example. You're starting your spending plan in January and the $1,200 property tax bill is also due in January, and you didn't account for this bill. Well, you're going to have to face that fact. It's going to be very stressful and upsetting. You may want to throw in the towel and go on a credit card binge. But trust me that this is a hurdle you will overcome.

Yes, there is no easy answer as to how to pay for the bill under these circumstances. But know, that once it's paid this time, ongoing, you just have to allocate $100/month for your property tax bill and you will never be in this situation again.

In this case, you might need to make a choice for this one month to live very simply, be willing to spend very small amounts in discretionary categories, and use the majority of discretionary money toward the property tax bill. Remember, **another month is coming. It's not forever**. It's one month.

And if you live that month one day at a time, and not focus on *Oh My God how can I not buy this, that, or the other*, for 31 days, it will be much more manageable, I promise. You can remind yourself that all is well in this moment, in this day, and that you can just get through this one day without spending. This is another place you will surely need support from others who have walked this path before you, and hopefully, a recovery program of some type you can turn to for help.

If it takes more than one month to get current, then you will just start dividing the bill up the month after you make the payment. So, maybe you will have nine months till it's due again. But if you persist, you will eventually get on an even keel with payments.

An Example

Let's say that the semi-annual car insurance is due in April. It's January, so what will you do? Well, it depends.

- If the bill is due on April 1, then you only have three months to accumulate the funds to pay the bill on time.
- So, you would divide $450, which is the total due, by three, and allocate $150 to that category in January, February, and March.
- Beginning in April, you will allocate 1/6th each month, which is $75.

Quarterly Bills

Before we end this lesson, I want to talk about quarterly bills because even I find this confusing. (I also went over this in the Foundational course). Quarterly bills are paid four times a year. Let's use quarterly taxes as an example because that is pretty straightforward. The bill is due on:

- January 15th
- April 15th
- July 15th
- October 15th

Where it gets confusing is how to accumulate for this. It's due four times a year, but you need to save up for it over three months. For example, let's say you owe $900 each quarter.

- If you divide the total you pay by three, you will consistently have the money to pay the tax bill.
- In this case, each month will be funded with $300.
- So, for instance, you will fund the money for July's bill in:
  - April
  - May
  - June

In practical terms, this means that in the month the bill is due (July, in this case), you will have accumulated $1,200 in the category. After you pay the $900 bill, you'll still have the July amount of $300 that goes toward October's payment.

If you are still unclear about this, please email me or post a question in the student discussion forum so I can explain it further.

Put Your Monthly Funding on Autopilot

If you use a software program like YNAB, you can pre-fund your categories for many months out. So, you don't have to spend any time manually entering these numbers each month, which could feel annoying if you are still resistant to this concept. Just like with any other positive habit, with each day that goes by where you engage in this practice, it becomes more and more a part of your life. So, each day, you don't look longingly at the money accumulating in these categories to pay your bills like a dog with a sirloin steak dangling in front of his face, you are giving yourself an amazing gift of peace.

Remember though, this accumulating money is not available for other uses. It's not a holding category for a free-for-all spending binge. **You need to consider this money already spent.** You need to tell yourself every time you are tempted to use it that it's not your money to spend.

In the next lesson, I'm going to give you a tip that can help you with this.

• LESSON #8 •

Romancing Temptation

IT'S DANGEROUS TO ROMANCE OUR compulsion. By that, I mean we need to find a way not to give in when faced with temptation. And it's far easier to stop before we begin to lust for something we want to buy than after we've gotten those juices flowing.

There's a remarkable, simple practice that can help with this. Just like the spending plan, it's not a replacement for some type of recovery program, but it is an amazing adjunct that I've incorporated into my own life and have found it incredibly helpful.

It's called practicing the three second rule, and it can really begin to help you shift your thinking. It's also referenced by Claire Weekes in the book "Hope and Help for Your Nerves" as not shooting yourself with the second arrow.

In Weekes' book, she writes that we cannot stop the first arrow of anxiety from hitting us. I translate that to be the first look or thought about something we want to buy.

But, she posits, we can stop from shooting ourselves with the second arrow or allowing ourselves to ruminate and obsess about it. The three second rule is a simple method to put her idea into practice.

Here's what you do: when temptation crosses your path, whether as a thought in your mind, an online ad, a store window, a tv show, a sale flyer, etc., instead of engaging with it, you turn away within three seconds.

So, in practice, if I walk by a store and see a pair of shoes that triggers desire, but I know I don't have enough money to buy shoes today, I literally walk away from it and, most importantly, don't allow my mind to obsess about it, or, what I call "romance" it. Every time the thought of those shoes comes into my mind, within three seconds, I literally pull a new thought about something unrelated into my mind. So, for instance, I wouldn't think about how much I love red, *and oh, wow, it's the color of those shoes*. No. I mean, I might think about what I'm going to do later that day.

Three seconds is long enough for something to cross your path, and for you to recognize that trouble's a brewin', yet not so long that you are being strangled by the python of desire. Here's what happens to me if I don't turn away physically <u>and</u> mentally.

Falling Down a Rabbit Hole

I keep looking at it, or thinking about it, desire increases, imagination runs wild, and my mind begins it's increasingly loud inner urging to scratch this itch!

And then, the disingenuous rationalization begins.

Oh, but those shoes will go perfectly with that outfit I'm going to wear to the party. Oh no, it's only on sale till the end of the day. Maybe I can forgo going out to eat with my friends for the rest of the month. Hmm, but then, wait, um, oh, maybe I can pay the electric bill late.

Oh wait, look at that sign in the window! I can get instant credit AND it's 30% off! WHOA. My credit's still good enough, I think, that I bet I can do it.

And it's not really debting if I get the instant credit, and then pay it off before it's due. I mean that's 30 days from now and I'm sure I'll figure out how to pay for the shoes by then.

And then, let's say I walk into the store with my brilliant new plan. They have the shoes in my size, they fit like a glove, and now, I'm at the checkout counter. What can possibly go wrong?

Well, I don't get the instant credit.

Sorry.

But now, I'm blinded by both embarrassment and desire, so I use my debit card or write a check for those shoes and don't even think about the repercussions of my actions ... at least not until I've come home or maybe, the next morning, when I'm wracked with guilt for doing it again.

But, I go put on my party outfit and try on those shoes, and the perfection of this coordinated outfit takes my breath away. So, there's no taking back the shoes.

Postscript: The party is so crowded that no one notices my shoes anyway.

And there you have it.

So, I find it's better to just walk away, throw out the ad, close out the website, watch another channel, and direct my mind elsewhere, rather than risking what happens if I romance temptation.

• LESSON #9 •

Keeping Track of Your Numbers

AS YOU GO THROUGH YOUR day, and spend money, you need a way to keep track of what you've spent so you can enter the transactions into your spending plan, whether that's written on an envelope, in a spreadsheet, or in budgeting software.

I keep a composition notebook and use a page a day to write down my spending. Here's a sample page:

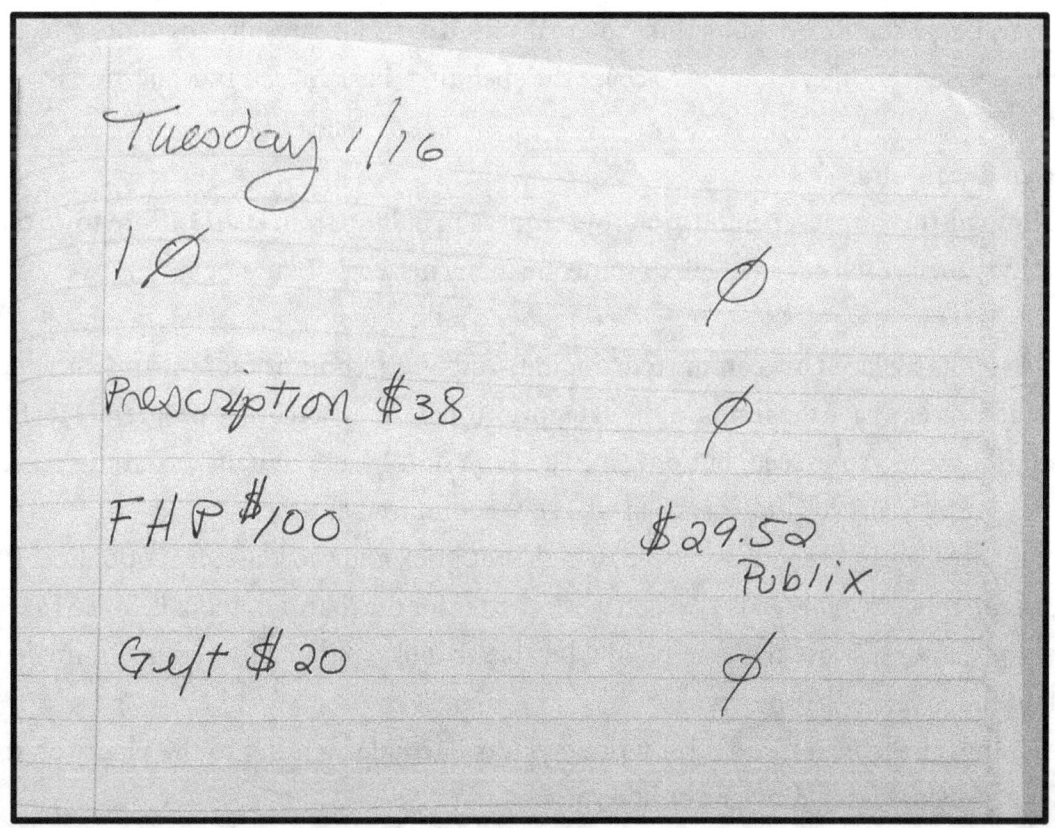

SUSAN B.

In the morning, I write down what I plan to spend and later in the day, what I actually spent. It's an excellent practice to give some thought to your spending for the day before you get going. You don't have to be precise in your planned numbers, but even approximating will be helpful.

When you go out and shop, you can either:

- Carry a notepad with you and write down each transaction
- Keep receipts together in your wallet
- Enter the transactions directly into a budgeting app or in a note app on your phone

Here is my basic daily spending plan process:

1. In the morning, I go to a new page in my composition notebook and date it with today's date.
2. I write down how much I anticipate in any income.
3. Then, I write down each category I may spend in and approximately how much I plan to spend. As part of this process, I check to ensure there is enough money left in that category for the spending. If not, I either don't buy it or see if there is another discretionary category from which to take the money.

    However, I urge caution in doing this. You really need to think carefully about the effects of taking money from another category to cover the spending. I ask myself two questions:

    1. Can it wait, and
    2. How will this impact spending in the category I'm pulling from - can I afford to do that? (I may even reach out to speak to someone in my network if I'm not sure.)

4. I do my best not to exceed my committed amount, and often, commit more than I anticipate spending as long as I have the funds in the category. As part of my recovery program, I do have a small buffer that I can exceed, but only if necessary. And I have actually asked the grocery cashier to remove items so I didn't exceed what I've committed at times.
5. I go through my day and spend as needed, whether at brick and mortar stores or online. Personally, I keep receipts in my wallet, which works better for me than a notebook. Since I spend cash so rarely, even if I lose the receipts, I'll be able to look up the transactions in my bank account online to verify the amounts.
6. In the evening, or the next morning, I write down my actual spending to the penny on that page in the notebook, including any online spending.
7. Then, at least a few times a week, I enter the transactions into my budgeting software.
8. And I generally reconcile with my bank account, which I will cover a few lessons from now.

I've created a video showing my entire process with my actual YNAB spending plan. The time stamps for each part of the process are in the video notes.

I've left out a few actions I additionally do every day because they are Twelve Step recovery-specific, and may not be necessary for you. But I'd be happy to share them with you if you send me an email and ask.

Practicing Delayed Gratification

There is another practice I engage in that has been crucial in helping me develop the ability to live with delayed gratification. If something I hadn't planned to buy suddenly appears in my day, I do the following:

1. First, I think about whether it can wait until the next morning when I make my new plan. As a compulsive spender, I am easily triggered to buy something that comes into view. Ninety nine percent of the time, if it's clothing, art supplies, or another triggering want, I generally wait until tomorrow.
   That way, it gives me time to get away from it, to step back, and see if it's just another bright and shiny object (which it usually is) or if it's a wise spending decision. And by the way, if I feel that urgent "gotta have it" feeling, I <u>definitely</u> wait!
2. If it can't wait (such as if I need gas), I make sure I have the money available in the category before proceeding. If it's an emergency, and I'm able to do so, I will actually reach out to someone to talk through how to handle it if I don't have enough money in the category to cover it.

Again, I'm only sharing my process. Doing these additional steps works for me. But, of course, they're optional for you.

Now, I didn't address tracking automatic withdrawals from your bank account, such as entertainment sites, insurance, and utilities. I'll give you some thoughts on those types of transactions in the next lesson.

• LESSON #10 •

Automatic Withdrawals and Deposits

EVEN IF YOU PRIMARILY USE envelopes to track your spending, there may be a few occasions where you have automatic withdrawals from your bank account as well as deposits.

First, I strongly suggest that you make a list of all your recurring transactions and the date when they are due to occur. If you are using the workbook from the Foundational course, you can add a note in worksheet #2 next to the name of the bill that will be auto-debited. Maybe just put the letters "AD." If you use an online calendar, such as Google Calendar, you can set up a repeating event for the appropriate time frame as a reminder. Once you have done this, it's important that you put a process in place to keep track of these transactions to ensure you have money available to pay for them.

Create Repeating Transactions in Budgeting Software

If you use YNAB, for instance, you can create transactions that repeat. (Screenshot next page.)

You can select from a number of timings, monthly, among them. Then, each month, on the date you select, the transaction will automatically show up in the transaction section. And YNAB shows you a grayed-out version of the upcoming transaction for the next month if you have enabled scheduled transactions to display from the filter.

I recommend setting up repeating transactions a few days to a week prior to when they will occur for a couple of reasons. First, it is easy to forget that an automatic transaction will occur, especially if

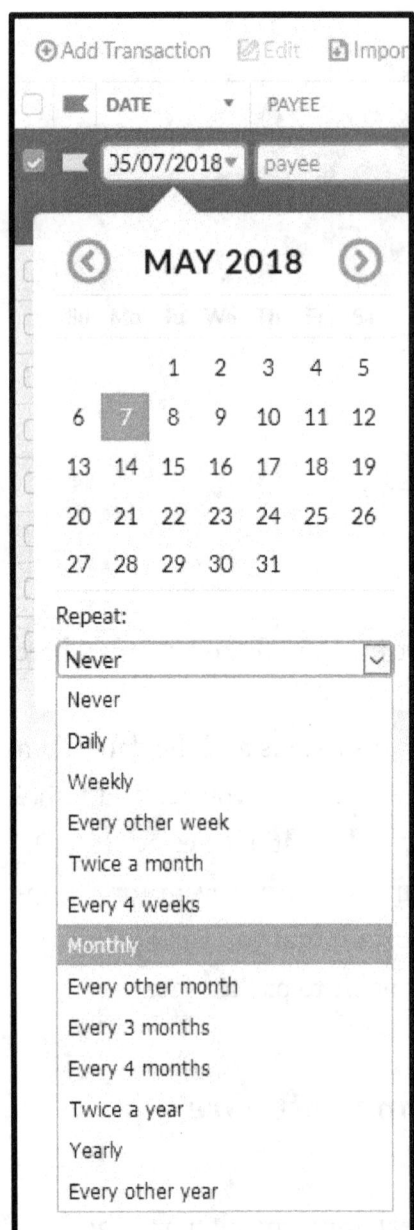

you are new this process. Having more lead time will help you be prepared as you begin working with your spending plan.

Second, automatic transactions don't always occur on the exact date specified. I've had them come out a day or two early. You don't want an unpleasant surprise around these transactions. And they can also hit your account a day or two late. But there's no problem for them to sit among your transactions.

Set Up Repeating Transactions for Income Too

You can follow the same process for regular income you receive. Just set it to repeat for whatever duration is appropriate. If you're using YNAB, be sure to enter the amount in the Inflow (not the Outflow) or it will throw off your totals. I can't tell you how many times I've accidentally entered income as spending or vice-versa. An easy mistake, but we are about to talk about reconciling, and if you follow my instructions, it will be a snap to see and correct such errors.

So, to sum up, if you are using budgeting software and can automate these recurring transactions, or set them up using an online calendar, you don't have to micro-manage them by writing them down. But however you track them, you need to be mindful of all transactions that go in or out of your bank account.

• LESSON #11 •

Reconciling

RECONCILING IS THE SECRET SAUCE that makes your spending plan reliable and accurate. If you learn the proper way to reconcile your spending plan with your bank accounts, you will always be able to trust that the amounts in your categories are truly available to spend.

People find reconciling a complicated topic. But once you understand the concept and learn an easy method to actually perform this task, you'll see that it's much simpler than you think.

After listening to this lesson, I invite you to watch the video I created showing my spending plan process. I've put time stamps where I begin reconciling in the video notes.

As you listen to this lesson, you may want to have the lesson text available as there are a number of screen shots.

Reconciling is simply a process to match your spending and income to your bank account. Essentially, it's just marking each transaction in your spending plan that has cleared your bank account. There are so many possible paths to vagueness and error. Here are just a few:

1. The bank charges you a fee mistakenly
2. The bank accidentally allows a fraudulent transaction to go through
3. You or the bank transpose a number so the transaction isn't accurately entered
4. You enter a number incorrectly
5. You enter a transaction multiple times
6. You forget to enter a transaction
7. You enter income as spending or vice versa

Please Don't Link Bank Accounts with Your Spending Plan Software

I urge students NOT to link their spending plan software with their bank accounts. Especially if you are a compulsive spender, you need the added clarity manually entering your transactions into the software or spreadsheet brings.

If you simply auto-download transactions, you have to review them anyway to match them to actual spending to check for the first three types of errors I mentioned earlier. Plus, you have to be sure the auto-selected category is actually the one you want to use. Not to mention the anxiety about security breaches that are all too real. Why even take a chance when manually entering transactions will take no more time to enter, and maybe less?

So, I'm going to proceed with the assumption that you have disconnected your banks with your budgeting software or never attached them to begin with. And I'm going to use YNAB for my examples, but the principles are the same no matter how you track your spending.

How Often to Reconcile

It is best to reconcile at least three times a week. I suggest you do this every day until you feel comfortable with the procedure, because you will have less transactions to deal with in a session. Once you have followed these steps a few times, you'll see it only takes about a minute or two to complete the procedure.

However, if you only reconcile weekly, monthly, or less often, I promise you this will become a spider web entrapping you in hours of trying to figure out where a small error occurred.

Adjustments to Your Spending Plan are a Nuclear Option!

And this brings me to one crucial caveat. If your budgeting software allows you to make an adjustment if you are off, I implore you not to take that seemingly easy route. Take it from my hard-won experience that it will come back to haunt you later. Making an adjustment (or starting fresh) should be the last resort for only the most dire spending plan mess. I promise you that if you follow my instructions, the likelihood of not finding an error is infinitesimal! Note that I never said you won't *find* errors. You *will* find errors, but it won't happen often. And I never said you won't *make* errors. But I further promise that, when you do, you will be able to figure it out easily.

What Number Gets Compared?

This is a screenshot of bank transactions. You'll note that there is an amount for the transaction and to the right of that is the available balance, which is also called the cleared balance. That shows you how much is available to spend in the account after deducting the transaction.

DATE ▼	DESCRIPTION	AMOUNT	BALANCE
4/18/2018	WITHDRAW AMAZON.C %% Card 30	($11.50)	$12,968.69
4/17/2018	WITHDRAW PAYPAL *AR Date 04/17/ %% Card 30	($45.28)	$12,980.19
4/17/2018	WITHDRAW PAYPAL *AR Date 04/17/ %% Card 30	$29.23	$13,025.47

Available Balance vs. Current Bank Balance

If a transaction has reached the bank, but it has not cleared, it means the bank is still waiting to get the final approval (for instance a check may take some time to clear). Sometimes, an account will show you these transactions with the word "pending" or "processing" next to the transaction. Some banks leave the balance blank if the transaction hasn't cleared.

But some banks also show you the current balance, which *includes* the pending transactions. This is what the example above would look like if the current balance displayed.

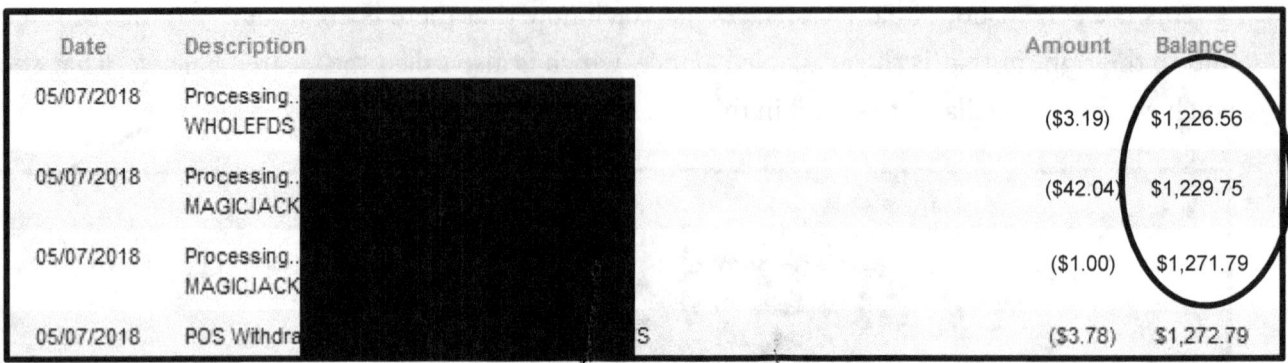

Pending Check Example

Let me give you another example. If your available balance is $600 and you see a check you wrote for rent for $400 showing up as pending, the current balance in your account (which includes the check) would be $200, which is the cleared balance of $600 minus the pending check of $400. As soon as the check clears, the Current balance *and* Cleared balance will both be $200.

Date	Description	Amount	Balance	Notes
5/7/18	Rent Check #328 (pending)	($400)		Current balance is $200 ($600-$400 = $200)
5/6/18	Publix Grocery	($35.83)	$600	Available balance = $600

Now, if you spend $600 before the check clears without putting more money into your bank account, you'll be overdrawn when the $400 check clears the bank.

Income Example

Let's take an income example. Remember, with a pending income transaction, you can't use the funds until it has cleared the bank. In this example, your cleared balance is $350. Your $1,000 paycheck is pending. So the current balance is $1,350. But if you write a check and spend $1,350 before the paycheck has cleared, you'll overdraw your account.

Date	Description	Amount	Balance	Notes
5/7/18	Paycheck (pending)	$1,000		Current balance is $1,350 $350 + $1,000 = $1,350
5/6/18	Publix Grocery	($35.83)	$600	Available balance = $600

The bottom line is that if you see pending transactions and the current balance is shown, the bank is essentially saying that if all goes well and, in this case, this paycheck clears, yes, you will have $1,350 available.

Use the Available Balance for Reconciling

For purposes of spending, you always want to consider the current balance that takes into account all pending transactions. But, for purposes of reconciling your spending plan, you *only* want to consider the available balance. That's because you are marking transactions in your spending plan that have cleared the bank.

In the first example I showed you with the pending $400 rent check, the available balance is $600. Therefore, you wouldn't mark that $400 check transaction in your spending plan as having cleared your bank account.

YNAB's Three Types of Balances

Here is YNAB's terminology for balances:

- Cleared Balance = Bank available balance
- Uncleared Balance = Total of all pending transactions
- Working Balance = Bank's current balance, which includes all transactions, pending and cleared.

When you reconcile, what you will be doing is ensuring that the cleared balance in your budgeting program or spreadsheet equals the bank's available Balance.

Clearing Transactions

In order to determine whether the cleared balance in your budgeting program or spreadsheet matches the available balance in your bank account, you need to check whether each transaction you have entered has already cleared the bank.

1. First, enter all outstanding transactions in your spending plan software. If you do this every day or two, the reconciliation process will take just a minute or two.
2. Next, go to your bank account online and view your transactions. You may want to print the screen if you have a lot of transactions to clear.
3. Open your spending plan software or spreadsheet as well.
4. Then, look at each uncleared transaction in your spending plan software or spreadsheet and compare it to the bank statement. If you find the transaction, you mark it cleared in your spending plan. If you use YNAB or a similar program, there is actually a field to clear your transaction. In YNAB, you click a gray letter "C" to the right of your transaction. Click it and it turns green, to show the transaction has cleared your bank account.

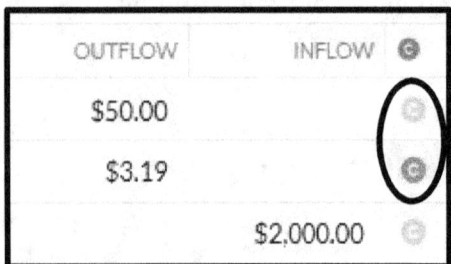

5. Then, if you have printed out your bank statement, put a check mark next to the transaction.
6. Continue with steps four and five for all uncleared transactions in your spending plan. If you find a cleared transaction in your bank statement that is not in your spending plan, check to see if you accidentally forgot to enter it or if it was previously cleared or reconciled.
7. Once you have reached the end of all uncleared transactions in your spending plan, you then check to ensure that the cleared balance in your spending plan is equal to the available balance in your bank account.

Checking for Errors

If your spending plan's Cleared Balance DOES NOT equal the Bank's available balance, then you need to go back through each transaction you entered to find the mistake.

In YNAB, for example, it could simply be that you accidentally didn't press the "c" for a transaction or mistakenly pressed it for a transaction that hadn't yet cleared. Maybe you transposed numbers and didn't catch that.

But here's the thing, you only need to go back to check as far as the last time your cleared balance equaled your bank's available balance to find the error. So, if you do this process consistently and often, you will only have a few transactions to check for errors. There is one exception to this. If you already cleared and reconciled a transaction and then you mistakenly enter the transaction a second time not remembering you did this, it could be the cause of your error.

In YNAB, after you reconcile (which I'll finish explaining in a moment), you will only have to go back as far as the most recent locked transaction to find the error, because the account was reconciled from that point back. By locked transaction, I mean that YNAB replaces the green "c" for cleared with a lock for every transaction that was both cleared and accounted for when you reconcile. If you watch my daily process video, it should clear up any confusion you may experience.

Budgeting software will have a button for you to press to complete the reconciliation process. So, for instance, in YNAB, when you have finished clearing transactions and YNAB's Cleared Balance equals the bank's available balance, you will click the Reconcile button to complete the process. When you do so, all the green C's next to cleared transactions will turn into locks.

If you are doing this manually in a spreadsheet or on paper, you will have to develop your own system to show which transactions have cleared and which have been reconciled. I suggest that you put a check mark next to each cleared transaction and a slash through the check mark to show it is cleared. Or an x for each cleared transaction with a circle around it if it's been reconciled.

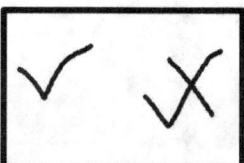 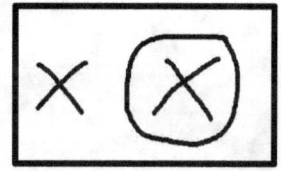

Note to YNAB users: If your transactions disappear from view after you've reconciled them, check the filter to be sure you are showing Reconciled Transactions.

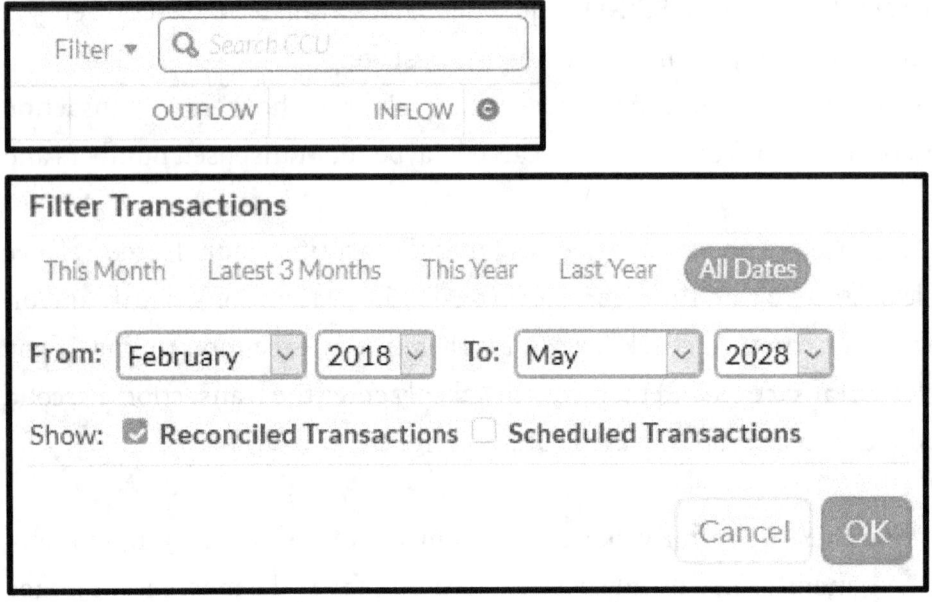

• LESSON #12 •

Dealing with Cash

I DON'T KNOW ABOUT YOU, but cash is my nemesis, even in recovery. Left to my own devices, I would be completely vague about how much cash I have. Honestly, I still am a lot of the time. I tend to lose cash, which is why I keep as little of it around as I can.

But you have to try to stay clear with your cash because it is part of your money. Most people need to use cash sometimes and since our goal is to do what we can to prevent vagueness, it's best to begin cultivating the habit of staying clear with cash and counting it up regularly. Right now, I have $14.87 in cash. I know this because I reconciled my cash recently.

Yes, you can reconcile your cash. You use the same principle as you do with money in the bank.

I've actually created two videos showing how I deal with cash in YNAB. But when I get cash, I can immediately clear it because, well, I'm the bank.

I generally keep my cash in a box. And every few weeks, I count up all the cash in the box and match it to the amount of cash my spending plan says I should have.

The Glorious Lost and Found Category

Now, here's a tip: I created a category called "Lost and Found." I funded it with $25 initially. Just one time. Because I still lose cash, if the amount of cash is less than the amount in my spending plan, I just take it from the Lost and Found category to create an adjustment. If I have more cash (which does happen rarely), I adjust the spending plan putting the overage back into the Lost and Found category. That way, I don't have to fund it again down the road and I don't spend more than five minutes trying to figure out why there's a discrepancy!

The problem I have experienced is that if I don't do this at least once a month (but really more often is optimal), the disparity can get very out of whack. But if you put just a bit of money into a lost and found category, you don't have to beat yourself up (which you shouldn't anyway) for 25 cents you can't find, or spend precious time searching for the error.

However, you don't want to do this with your bank account, as I explained in a previous lesson, because bank records are precise and not matching the available balance to your spending plan's cleared balance could mean the difference between solvency and being hit with an insufficient funds fee!

I talked about cash in an earlier lesson, but it's worth revisiting here, now that you've come so far. As I said, you must account for your cash in your spending plan and you need to track the pennies. And not round up.

This is a sore spot with many compulsive spenders. The thing is, we want to be clear about our money. And, like it or not, pennies, dimes, nickels, and quarters do make up dollars. Think about it. Would you like it if the bank eliminated the pennies? So, if you get a check for $297.45, they only give you $297. Or what if a store rounded up? So, for instance, if a pair of shoes costs $89.58, they didn't want to deal with change and charged you $90. Would you like that?

Over time, that change you receive and spend makes a big difference. And getting clear with your spending means getting clear with all your spending. When you are actually using the spending plan, you'll understand that what your spending plan says is available must match what the bank shows as available in order for your spending plan to be useful. Please trust me that rounding up or down is going to eventually lead to vagueness, which is dangerous for a compulsive spender. If you can't trust the accuracy of your spending plan, well, it's pretty much useless. However, because we are human and prone to error, in the case of cash, it is reasonable to have a way to cover a small shortfall rather than expending precious energy chasing the error.

SECTION III:

RELATIONSHIPS AND MONEY

• LESSON #13 •

Your Partner and the Spending Plan

THERE ARE UNIQUE CHALLENGES AROUND effectively working with a spending plan when it comes to dealing with money and relationships. It's been proven that money squabbles can actually lead to divorce. A 2009 study showed that couples who reported disagreeing about finance once a week were over 30 percent more likely to get divorced than couples who reported disagreeing about finances a few times a month.

Among the issues that can affect any couple are:

1. Your partner spends excessively
2. Your partner lives in deprivation due to fear and expects you to do the same
3. Disagreements on where to spend money, such as on a bigger house, type of car, etc.

However, there are multiple layers to the difficulties when you commit to living by a spending plan (and especially if you are in a recovery program) that don't affect couples otherwise. Here are three scenarios:

1. Both partners are compulsive spenders/debtors and only one makes the commitment to live by the spending plan.
2. Only one partner is a compulsive spender/debtor and that is the person who commits to living by the spending plan.
3. A third scenario, where both partners are committed to recovery, will still have hurdles, but they will be different as they are on the same path.

In the first two cases, a common phenomenon is that the partner who hasn't made the commitment feels threatened by the efforts of the other. Change, even for the better, can feel scary, an upsetting of the status quo, no matter how dysfunctional the couples' financial life was beforehand. Even with a "normal" spending partner, there may be efforts to thwart or sabotage the recovery efforts, which may not be conscious.

As an example, I, myself have had issues with my spouse, who is very frugal, and actually writes down everything he spends, rounding up to the nearest dollar, as a matter of habit. However, he has, at times, become extremely frustrated with me because I choose to account for spending to the penny. Such a small thing, right? But is it really about the pennies?

For me, it's important that I stick to what works for me, no matter what, but to remember that there is pain in change, not just for me, but for those whom it affects. This is where patience is important, and remembering that this person also put up with me when I was in full-fledged compulsive spending mode. Accept that you may feel guilt when your partner gets angry at your new "cheap" attitude or when you say you need to wait when a discretionary purchase suddenly comes up.

Here are some tips from my own and others' experience, strength, and hope about how to effectively and successfully work with your spending plan and maintain your sanity when you have a partner.

1. Take responsibility for managing the household money. By this, I mean that you should maintain the spending plan. In my home, my husband and I have separate accounts and we each pay our own bills, so this is easy. However, in homes where money is combined, there will be a bit more complexity, which I will get to shortly.

    Let's face it, if your partner has been handling the money and it was working out well, then you wouldn't need this training program, would you? If possible, I recommend that you take over the responsibility of managing the household. This provides you with the most clarity and often, the partner is actually relieved to let go of this task.

    At first, partners who are not compulsive spenders, but who have had to live through the consequences of, and pay the price for, your own out of control spending, are excited and hopeful that life will become balanced and the insanity will come to an end. However, if you are truly committed to recovering from compulsive spending as well as maintaining the spending plan, inevitably, there will come a point of resentment where the partner feels threatened by your new behavior shaking up the relationship or, maybe because the partner wants to purchase something and you need to set boundaries (especially if your partner is the only one working or an active compulsive spender). It can be very challenging, and sometimes, the partner simply takes the money and uses it anyway

This is an opportunity to practice patience, remembering that our partners have put up with our addiction for years. One thing we learn in Twelve Step recovery is that we cannot control others. In cases like this, though it may evoke panic, we can seek support to help us work through these issues and to help us learn patience and acceptance. Again, that's why I urge you to seek out a Twelve Step recovery program, which can give you the tools you need to withstand these challenges and recovery from compulsive spending. It's admittedly much harder to stay strong in your convictions if you are being pummeled and have nowhere to turn for help.

2. Even if you are not working and are given money each month from your partner, or your partner doesn't want to give up the control, you can still create a spending plan for the items you buy using the same Fearless Budgeting principles.

3. In cases where you have told your partner how much was available for a purchase and the partner spends more, the same principles apply. For instance, if the partner takes your children out to lunch and you say there is $30 available in the restaurants category, but they spend $45, all you can do is adjust the spending plan and recognize that this wasn't your choice.

4. As I said earlier, my husband and I keep our money separate. I take care of my own bills, such as long-term care insurance, clothing, medical, etc. But we each pay for certain joint items during the month, and on the first of the next month, we "settle up" our accounts and reimburse the other. Bear in mind that I would have already allocated this money to the respective categories so it's available. Here are a few examples of possible scenarios:

- He sends a check for the utilities and I pay my half on the first of the next month.
- I buy all the food and he gives me a flat amount to offset my payment for the utilities.
- We may alternate who buys stamps so no reimbursement is necessary.
- I buy air filters for the air conditioner and he pays me his half on the first of the next month.

What if You Find Out Your Partner Struggles with Spending?

This may sound strange, but I have seen it happen. Sometimes, you have been so consumed with your own out of control spending that you don't realize, until you begin working with your spending plan, that your partner has money issues as well. In fact, you may have thought the money problems were all due to your behavior, but you may come to see that your partner is not the bastion of sober spending that you thought.

But here is where you need to become even more committed to this new way of life, and again, why a recovery program can be the key to healing your own addiction as well as your relationship. It's vital that you continue to focus on your own recovery and not give up. This is going to take a rigorous commitment because it's much harder to stay strong in the face of relationship challenges, which may make us want to escape through spending.

Please be mindful of not hammering your partner, as you must know from your own experience that this does not work. All you can do is to keep tracking your numbers and working with your spending plan to the best of your ability. If you are in a recovery program, throw yourself even harder into it, giving service and asking for support. And, if you are spiritually-focused, continue to pray for your partner to find peace around spending.

• LESSON #14 •

Children and Your Spending Plan

WHEN YOU MAKE A COMMITMENT to living within your means and by a spending plan, all the relationships in your life will be affected. Children will need to get used to the new parent who will no longer feed their every spending whim.

Guilt is inevitable. So, accept that you may feel some guilt and pain when your children weep over your cruel refusal to buy them what they want the moment they want it. (I hope you realize I'm being facetious here.)

I've never really understood why money was such a taboo subject. But I suppose if I think about the shame I have suffered over my own behavior with money, it is more understandable. However, I've seen many who were not addicts around money still keep tight-lipped, which makes it seem as if managing money is a mystical and mysterious skill. But the fact is that dealing with money is something we do nearly every day! If we don't talk to our children about money in a personal way, how on earth are they expected to learn how to manage it when they grow up?

It's funny, I was just about to write that I've always been honest with my now-adult son about money. But then, I realized that I certainly wasn't honest when I debted to buy him the newest game system every year or a myriad of other trinkets that I couldn't afford.

I'm grateful that my husband has always been responsible with money and that I got into recovery while my son was young enough to benefit from my experience, strength, and hope. Not young, he was about 18 years old, but it's never too late to become a better role model for your children. And, gratefully, it did make a positive impact on him.

It's a shame that finance 101 isn't taught in school. What a difference that would make if an entire generation of young people learned from the start how to live within their means.

So, now, let's talk about children and money.

If you are like I was when I was actively debting and spending, you can't bear the thought of your children feeling pain or lack. While nearly all my son's friends' parents were wealthy, I was always living hand to mouth to credit card. But he had every new toy that he wanted and never had to yearn for that toy because I always bought it before any pain point.

Now, in recovery, I have learned that not giving in to my son's every whim would have actually been the greatest gift I could give him. Gratefully, there was still time in our case, to change the dynamic. Once we got over the initial hurdles around the shift in our financial relationship, he began to take pride in insisting that he wanted to pay for things that I offered to pay for instead.

It really was in the nick of time that I got sober with money because he was just finishing high school and about to go to college. I still had some authority over his money and was able to judiciously choose (with the help of my Twelve Step support system) what I would and would not pay for. As an added gift, I was able to talk with him about these issues as well. And to stay calm and committed in the face of the brilliant "legal arguments" only a teenager can concoct followed by pouting, anger, and guilt to convince me to change my mind.

By the way, I wrote an article for a magazine called "The Billfold" about what happened when my son went to college.

So, here are some tips to help you with your children:

1. When your children cry that it isn't fair when you have to (or choose to) say no to them, remember that pain is part of growth, for all of you. Maybe you can help them save toward the goal or ask them to save for half and you will pay the other half when they have enough, if your spending plan can accommodate that.
2. Remember the "Lost and Found" category I had you create to offset losing or finding change. Well, as you help your children develop better money habits, this category can also offset other types of inevitable errors that can occur. For instance, if you give them money for an item, expecting change later, and the correct amount isn't returned, you have a buffer of money to make sure your spending plan is accurate.
3. You may want to additionally create a category with a small amount of money for library fines. If you have more than one child and they take out lots of library books, it may be unmanageable for you to keep track of when they are due. You might take it out of their allowance if they are old enough to be responsible. However, these aren't your books and not your debt. So, you may decide when or if this is a good learning experience for them around responsible money management.
4. Talk to your children about your spending plan. When you say yes and when you say no, use the opportunity to help them understand what a spending plan is and the importance of living within one's means.

5. What if you have more than one child and one receives a money gift but the person giving the gift accidentally forgot to give it to the other as well. How do you handle such a situation? There are a number of options (and maybe more I haven't thought about!):

- You *could* give the forgotten child the money, yourself. But then, would you need to deprive yourself in another category to do so? If so, you may want to think about whether you would be giving your child the right message.
- You might explain the situation to the child and maybe plan a special time together to make up for it. While that may not totally satisfy your child, you are gently helping them learn the painful lesson that life can sometimes be unfair. But softening the blow with a non-money experience.
- You may consider speaking to the giver about the situation, which could potentially cause embarrassment or even defensiveness if the giver insists that no one was left out. On the other hand, maybe the giver would want to know and make it right.
- Finally, you might have the other child or children split their money with the one left out so they all learn a lesson in sharing.

As you can see, there is no cut and dried answer, and each choice involves some pain. But there are valuable lessons to be learned by each option. Teaching our children about managing money and living within their means is a vital lesson they will never learn in school. It is truly up to us, as parents, to impart to them what we are learning in recovery.

The tool of a spending plan and record keeping, if you share it with your children, may make an impression you never imagined. My son proudly told me right after college that he was tracking all his cash spending with a phone app. I never thought he was paying attention, but he was. And he still tracks his money years later.

As a senior in college, though he initially wasn't going to get a credit card, he eventually decided to do so because he felt it would help him establish credit. He's now 27 and is insistent that he does not want to live beyond his means. Wow. So, far, so good, right?

But, I still hold my breath, worried that the compulsive spending gene has been passed on to him and will strike unexpectedly. I need to let go and remember that this is his path, not mine. And that is my last tip. Even though we can teach our children, we cannot make their mistakes for them. We certainly made ours. They must follow their own path. But the hope is that by being open about our mistakes and, now, our commitment to making better choices around our spending, we can, at the least, help them see how to avert financial disaster.

• LESSON #15 •

When Parents Give Us Money

IT'S NOT EASY WHEN AS adults, we have always been given money by our parents, to say no once we are committed to living within our means. And maybe the better choice for you is to continue accepting their gifts.

However, if you now see that the price you have paid by taking money from your parents is to leave you feeling stuck, manipulated, angry, embarrassed, or humiliated, you may want to work on learning to let go. The fact is, there are few issues so deep as those involving our parents and money.

In the practical sense, it is not so easy to say no to money when you are in a difficult situation. But again, if accepting the gift is a spider web of strings and keeps you stuck, then maybe you should consider breaking the cycle, even if it is painful.

As with all addictive behavior, when the pain of accepting the gift becomes worse than the pain you are avoiding by taking it, you will be willing to face the challenge of saying no. Being in recovery from compulsive spending and debting doesn't mean we never feel pain. It means we have a level playing field and can face pain without engaging in our addictive behavior. You are the only one who knows, in recovery, if accepting financial gifts from your parents is enabling you to stay sick with money. Indeed, this is a complex issue and there is no one right answer.

In my own life, money was a horrible, divisive element in my relationship with my father. My father's only way to show love was through money, which he also resented. So, there was truly a mixed message throughout my growing up. I got everything I wanted, but there was hell to pay emotionally. My mom died when I was 26, and right after her death, he gave me thousands to buy furniture for my apartment, and continued to pay my rent, despite the fact that I was working.

But soon thereafter, he remarried a woman who convinced him to cut me off without a word. I didn't find out he had stopped paying for my health insurance until I got a letter from the company saying I was no longer covered and it was too late to reinstate the policy. That led to the conversation where my father angrily told me I was cut off. Just so. That's it. Leaving me bewildered by this new life for which I wasn't at all prepared, and an attitude by my father that left me feeling ashamed and humiliated. And that's why I did all I could to make the transition with my son as painless as possible, though not pain-free. It's scary to get cut off when you haven't been raised with this goal in mind, whether it happens all at once or over time.

Though it seems like it would have been much easier for me if my father weaned me off the financial wagon train gently after college ... or even high school, I'll bet that I would have been quite resentful no matter what ... because I was never taught financial responsibility.

But, it doesn't matter because that is not how it happened. It was only in recovery that I came to understand that, though I despised how it was done to me, it was truly for the best. And, thankfully, once I got sober with money, I learned how to take care of myself (and my son) because of it.

I know people who are afraid to say no to their parents' money offers because that will trigger parental anger, and yet, they're afraid to say yes because they know that will trigger other control issues by the parent. And, of course, this is not just limited to parents. Brothers and sisters, indeed any family member, can use money as a way to control us.

If you are serious about changing your relationship with money and your family, then here is some food for thought:

1. You will become willing to breaking old patterns and habits.
2. You *can* learn to stand on your own two feet.
3. If you do accept a financial gift, you can still set boundaries that do not inflict pain upon you.
4. You can learn to accept a financial gift with integrity and good feeling.
5. It will take time and work, but you'll eventually understand your own motivations about accepting money from your family.
6. You will discern whether you are being manipulative around family money, and take responsibility for it.
7. You'll gain clarity about whether accepting the gift is enhancing your recovery.
8. And, finally, whether you do or don't accept the gift, if the giving party still tries to manipulate and control you, you will see it for what it is and have compassion for them, instead of taking it personally and feeling ashamed.

In the next lesson, I'll talk about lending money.

• LESSON #16 •

Lending Money

THIS IS GOING TO BE a short lesson. The bottom line is ... don't lend money if you can't afford to lose it. I don't believe in lending money at all. If I can't give it to the person, I don't lend it to them.

As an avid viewer of the judge reality shows, and having been burned too many times when I wanted to boost my own ego by lending money I couldn't afford to lose, I've seen how this practice destroys relationships.

Living within your means and by a spending plan will be an invaluable aid in stopping this practice if you currently engage in it. And I no longer feel guilty or embarrassed to say no. It's ironic that in my compulsive spending days, I'd end up debting just to lend money.

That's insane, right?

Maybe I didn't think I'd debt, but when the person didn't pay me back and I was already living above my means, well, guess what? Out came the credit card to cover my shortfall.

So, I just thought this was important enough to make it a lesson on its own.

• L E S S O N # 1 7 •

Gift-Giving Tips

ONE OF THE HARDEST ASPECTS of recovery for many compulsive debtors and spenders is putting the brakes on extravagant (i.e., expensive) gift giving, especially around the holidays. The idea that more is not only better, but required, is a part of our disease that is fueled by the media and even those around us (think kids who may have gotten used to feeding the "gimme gimme" monster).

We who are so used to being the big spender, especially around holidays and gifts, find our whole sense of self tied up with giving the biggest and best gifts. But if we are committed to living within our means, then we get willing to sit through our discomfort, and change our perspective, as we actively live within our means around gift giving.

I know the first year of my recovery from compulsive spending was tantrum and tear-filled regarding gift-giving because there were limits. Even later on, I remember feeling really ashamed when a family member was hospitalized and I didn't have enough money accumulated in my gift category to buy her anything. I settled on calling a lot, and she was grateful, but when she'd share what others had sent her, it was hard to hear without beating myself up for not finding a way to buy her something. With more years of practice, I rarely feel that way, and am grateful for whatever I can give, and that I only give what I can.

So, here are some tips to help you stay sane with money and gift-giving:

1. Realistically fund your gift category for the next year. Make sure you think about all gifts you need, birthdays, holidays, etc. The miracle of the Debtors Anonymous concept of a pressure relief group (PRG) is that two others recovering from this addiction help you figure out what is reasonable to put away each month. If you are not in that recovery program, you can still elicit the help of people you trust who will not judge you. It's definitely best to get help around this issue, as it's really easy to convince yourself that you have to fund the gift category in a way that is out of balance with the rest of your wants and needs.

2. Stay in reality about what you can afford. For me, even now, I can no longer afford to spend much on gifts. If I deprive myself to buy gifts for others, my disease will eventually win and I will relapse. That is why the feedback of a PRG team helps me to see clearly how much is enough.
3. If your new gift-giving reality is far less than you hoped, and you begin to feel demoralized and upset as the holidays approach and you feel the pinch becoming a stranglehold, reach out to your support network to help you work through these feelings. They will pass. I promise.

    The miracle of being in a recovery program for compulsive spending and debting is that you can call others who have been through this challenge. Knowing you aren't alone (and that it will actually get better) can really help.
4. Who do you really need to buy gifts for? Maybe it's time to whittle down your list. I'm not trying to be Scrooge here, but sometimes, we just give as a knee-jerk reaction when in reality, it's not really necessary. For instance, someone I know said that when the nieces and nephews had graduated college and were on to their own adult lives, she didn't feel that she needed to continue giving them presents.
5. If you give Christmas gifts, consider shifting to a Secret Santa gift exchange with your family. Maybe you aren't the only one feeling the pinch of gift giving. Such a suggestion to pick one name each might bring a huge sigh of relief among the other members of the family.
6. Think about moving to charitable gifting in lieu of gifts. For instance, I know someone who sponsors a child in another country and has let her family know that is her holiday gift.
7. If you have children who are used to getting lots of really expensive holiday gifts, tamping down the spending may result in a lot of angst and button pushing to manipulate you. But during such times (and trust me, I have been there – it sucks), remember that you are teaching your children an invaluable lesson about the importance of living within one's means.

    Even if you get a negative response from an adult with whom you exchange gifts, or feel judged by them, remember that you are choosing to live in recovery and within your means. And the extravagance of the gift is not the gauge of how much we love people.
8. The holiday season is also a great opportunity to show your kids the real meaning of the season by participating in charitable acts, like volunteering in a soup kitchen, visiting a nursing home, and encouraging them to do other acts of kindness. In addition, this may be the perfect time to open a dialogue with your children about responsible spending, which could end up being a profound bonding and healing experience.
9. Consider making gifts. Do you have any art, writing, or crafting skills? Homemade gifts don't have to be "hokey." When my son was 21, I wrote a book for him and embedded

photographs. The only cost was a few dollars for printing. In the past, I debted hundreds and hundreds of dollars to get him the latest, greatest game system and more "stuff" for his birthday. But this was the first time he ever cried and hugged me with such emotion in response to receiving a gift from me.

The delight in his eyes showed me that he truly cherished the book. For his 25th birthday, I wasn't able to write much, so I made him a handmade book with short phrases and created art around it. For his 27th birthday, I made him a doll of his favorite author and a mini copy of part of his favorite book by that author. Actually, I bought an inexpensive Charles Darwin doll and morphed it into the author he loved. He thought it was the funniest gift ever.

If you feel you don't have any skills for making gifts, it's never too late to open yourself to learning how to create. I was artistically anorexic for my entire adult life. It was only after becoming disabled at the age of 55 and being told I needed to find a creative outlet that I began my artistic journey and came to discover my creative joy.

I cannot tell you how many arts and crafts I learned to do for free from watching videos and reading instructions online! Here are just a few of the skills I've learned from free videos and instructions:

- Hand sewing to convert a dress to shorts and skirts to pants
- Drawing intricate patterns (check out Zentangle.com especially if you think you cannot draw!)
- Crochet and knitting
- Tapestry weaving
- and lots more – all of which require minimal investment (I pretty much forget about any hobby that requires lots of money)

Any of these could provide lots of wonderful, thoughtful gifts to those you love at minimal cost. If you are feeling guilty, or self-conscious, or beating yourself up, or feeling less than, or drowning in desperation about holiday gift giving, then these last two tips are probably the most important of all:

1. Be grateful. The amazing thing about gratitude is that it is a gift we can give ourselves under all circumstances. We may not be happy today, but we can always be grateful. It is a good habit to write down a few gratitudes daily, but during the holidays it may be even more important as a gift to yourself.
2. Turn your thoughts to someone you can help. Giving service is the cornerstone of recovery from compulsive debting and spending.

SUSAN B.

Listening to a friend, spending time with someone who is infirm, driving a family member to an appointment, all of these are examples of how we can be generous without spending a penny. We each have an unlimited ability to give of ourselves in ways that cost nothing but mean so much to others. All we have to do is tap into it.

SECTION IV:

BONUS TIPS

• LESSON #18 •

Moving Money Between Categories

I WANT TO TALK ABOUT moving money between categories. Of course, you *can* do this. No one is stopping you. But if you don't treat your categories seriously, and with respect, it becomes easier to give in to whims and pull money from needs for wants. And before you know it, you stop tracking your numbers and end up compulsively spending again.

I've known people who worked hard for months to accumulate money in their buffer category, so they could live in the next month, and almost had enough to make it work, but they drained that buffer when a bright and shiny object compelled them to forget why they shouldn't spend all that money. If you recall, living in the next month means this month's income is spent next month, so you start on the first of the month with the entire month funded, no need to wait, in desperation, for the next paycheck.

Of course, if a true emergency arises, it's sensible to take money from other categories to cover it. And the miracle of working with the spending plan as you have learned in the Fearless Budgeting training program, is that you will inevitably accumulate money in discretionary categories over time. Though earmarked for one purpose, it can certainly be used for another under the right circumstances. For instance, maybe I let my clothing category build up over time to $600. But I needed $400 for the co-insurance to pay the emergency room doctor for my child's broken arm. That is a reasonable reason to re-allocate the money. I'm still left with $200 in my clothing category and feel grateful that I don't have to pull from savings or debt to take care of my child's health emergency.

And, so, in the next lesson, I want to talk about my best friend, delayed gratification.

• LESSON #19 •

Delayed Gratification

COMPULSIVE SPENDERS DESPISE DELAYED GRATIFICATION. We can't abide the pain it causes us. The literal feeling that we will die, just expire on the spot, if we don't buy it NOW.

This addiction is one of more, more, more ... and not enough. It calls to us through bright and shiny objects, education and training opportunities, career paths, non-life-threatening medical treatments not covered by insurance, gift-giving, and a whole lot more.

Buying makes us high, like a shot of adrenaline would. I don't know about you, but for me, the high is in the desire, culminating in the purchase. Once I have whatever I wanted so desperately ... meh. How many times have we bought something that we just had to have and then when we got it, it was a huge letdown. Or we didn't even open the box. Or we were excited for a brief period, but then arrived the next bright and shiny object to obsess about.

The thing is, for a compulsive spender, there is no ultimate ahhhhhhhhh. Right? How many times did we say, this, this is the final thing we're going to buy with a credit card? Or this is the last impulse to buy because now, our desire for [fill in the blank] will be satiated.

So, it's important to stop lying to ourselves about this characteristic. There is no ultimate ahhhhhh. Accepting that is important. If it's true that there's no ultimate ahhhhh, then it must also be true that waiting to buy, or even not buying at all, doesn't mean we're giving something up that will be our holy grail ... no matter what it is. Trust me, the desire will pass and a new object of desire will take its place whether you buy it or not.

I firmly believe that what's in my best and highest good is not to debt out of choice (remembering that for life-saving surgery, yes, even I would debt). So, now, when I'm faced with one of those spending decisions around something that makes me feel like it's the one thing that will change everything or makes me feel like I will die if I don't have it – if I can't afford it, then I know it's definitely NOT in my best and highest good even if my addict mind is trying to convince me that it is.

So, what to do. Here's where I'm putting in a plug, again, for Twelve Step recovery because that's the only way I know out of this. But I will tell you that the way out is practicing delayed gratification. However, without recovery, there is no way I would be willing to embrace the pain it can cause. Now, having made delayed gratification my friend, she's gifted me with the ability to:

1. Be able to pause and recognize when I'm in the grips of addictive desire.
2. Say no to making any decision until the desire has diminished. And this, my friends, can take months, though it often only takes hours or just a day or two.
3. Find the willingness to let go entirely if I don't have the money to pay for whatever it is. Or, I can choose to create a category for it and decide to re-allocate money from elsewhere or accumulate money in that category over time.

I remember seeing this somewhere, "Pain is what I walk through. Misery is what I sit in." I may feel disappointment if I realize I can't afford something that a salesperson has convinced me will change my life. But I go back to what I know and that's the fact that compulsive spending, impulse spending, and debting are never what's best for me. So, I can choose to either ruminate and build resentment. Or I can be thankful that I don't have to live with guilt and regret and shame over my purchases anymore.

Now, I truly practice this in my daily life. If something unexpected comes up, something completely discretionary, I wait until the next day to see if I still want it. And if I'm gripped by demanding desire, then I wait for it to simmer down. As I said earlier, I've never regretted waiting, and too often, I've regretted spending.

• LESSON #20 •

Dealing with Debt

I HAVE DELIBERATELY STAYED AWAY from the subject of credit cards and debt through this training program because it is a highly charged subject that impacts your spending plan for sure but isn't relevant to how you create and work with one.

But, now that you have your spending plan in place, I do want to talk about debting, and give you some suggestions.

I strongly suggest you go back now and listen to, or read, lesson #5 in the Foundational course, "Crucial Lesson Spending Plan vs. Budget," where I talk about my experience paying off debt, and as a pep talk to help you move forward.

First, let's talk about the debt you currently have. It's crucial that you understand that your creditors are not your higher power. They don't own you. I get really upset when I hear financial gurus talk about "pulling yourself up by the bootstraps" and applaud when people say they got out of debt by living in abject deprivation, as though they needed to punish themselves or do penance for incurring the debt. Such a philosophy would send me spinning out into a spending binge of epic proportions.

I know, as a compulsive spender, that if I add to the shame I already feel by continuing to punish myself, it will backfire. Now, that is vastly different than accepting limits around my spending and being responsible about repaying the debt. The key, again, is balance. The beauty of the pressure relief group in Debtors Anonymous is that you get help from others who have been where you are to make a decision about how much of your money can go to debt repayment without it becoming a punishment.

Many years ago, I paid off $22,000 in debt. I did that by paying $5 a month to creditors for years until I was able to make larger payments. They didn't like it one bit, but once they accepted that first $5 payment, at least in those days, I'm not sure about today, but back then, they couldn't get a judgment against me as long as I paid it every month on time.

We feel so guilty about our debts and the wreckage our behavior has caused that once we make the decision to make things right, we may fall into that trap of desperation to fix it immediately. But it doesn't work for people like us. It always backfires because we can only live in extremes for so long before we crack.

So, it's crucial you get honest with yourself and not try to pretend that you can do more than you realistically can do. It's that kind of big spender thinking that gets us in trouble! Turn to your support system to determine how much you can realistically pay on your debts.

And, by the way, if you are, or become, disabled, you may be able to get a reduction in your monthly payment without raising the interest rate for the life of the debt. That happened to me and it was truly a miracle. The creditor may turn you down, but it can't hurt to ask.

A Helpful Option

I do want to mention an option that you may want to consider. A debt management program can be very helpful in possibly reducing your monthly payments and interest. With a debt management program, you still pay the full balance of the debt and their fee is included in the monthly amount you pay (I believe there is also a small administrative fee to start the process as well). It is not the same as other types of debt reduction programs, which I don't recommend at all. I suggest you listen to episode 026 of the "I Can't Stop Spending!" podcast, where I interview Katie Bossler of Greenpath Financial Wellness, a wonderful non-profit organization that I highly recommend.

I wanted to interview someone from this company, in particular, because they are a company I trust. I know three people who were helped by GreenPath and got out of debt. In addition, I, myself, had two sessions with them, but by that point, I had already gotten the best deal I could on my own, so they weren't able to do anything more. However, I was very impressed with them.

But this is NOT just an interview. It's really a 40-minute seminar that will give you an exceptionally detailed understanding about the different ways debt can be paid off. I learned a lot from this interview – in particular, the difference between a debt management, debt consolidation, and debt settlement program.

I urge you to listen to this 42-minute podcast after this lesson. I think you will find it extremely helpful. See the resources handout for the link or just go to ICantStopSpending.com/026.

To Debt or Not to Debt ... That is the Question

So, now, what about the future use of unsecured debt? Well, my opinion is that if you are truly a compulsive spender, then I do not believe that you can handle credit cards responsibly.

I believe that you may tell yourself that you can. Or convince yourself that you can't get rid of them for reasons that your addict mind makes up, such as worry that an emergency will require their use or it will adversely affect your credit or that you get points or cash back for using them. I've used each of these excuses myself.

The problem is that keeping cards for a potential emergency, but being unable to stop using them for non-emergencies, means that the money that you could be accumulating in categories for a real emergency is being frittered away.

And if you are so tied into the points or cash back, then I urge you to consider the price you pay in impulse spending and the toll it takes on your health and relationships compared to the rewards you receive from having the cards.

A Tale from My Past

I'm not talking hypothetically. In my compulsive spending days, I still vividly remember my husband, who is definitely NOT a compulsive spender, enthusiastically encourage me to follow his lead and put all my daily expenses on the card ... and then pay it off at the end of each month.

What a great idea! And it was for month one. Month two felt more constricted. And by month three, I had well exceeded the amount for those daily expenses. And off to the races I went.

I ended up racking up over $34,000 in six years, a number that was inching uncomfortably close to exceeding my annual income.

The problem is that I lived in denial about my inability to say no to anything I wanted. Without the cards, let's face it, I'd still have the compulsion, but I wouldn't have had the means to wreak such havoc on my finances. I'll say that left untreated, though, my compulsive spending would still have destroyed me because I would have found a way to feed that monster. So, I'm grateful that I turned to the Twelve Step program to help me both close the accounts and lead me into recovery from the compulsion to spend.

Look, I remember the terror of closing those accounts, the nauseating anxiety of letting go. What if there was an emergency? Well, yes, there *have* been emergencies since I took the step to close all my credit card accounts in 2009, but the miracle is that I was able to find other ways to pay for them. It's always worked out without my having to debt because I was willing to do so. And sometimes I was willing to sit in the discomfort of not having a knee-jerk reaction, and came to see that what appeared to be an emergency wasn't after all.

The Thorny Issue of Medical Debt

But what if a medical emergency meant debting? That's a third rail topic that I can't fully address in this training course. But I will say that, while debt is debt, if I needed to incur unsecured debt at the hospital for life-saving surgery, of course I'd do it. But that is vastly different than *choosing* Care Credit for a discretionary medical procedure or treatment that my addict mind has convinced me is necessary and urgent, but my rational mind knows is not. Discretionary means that I can choose to accumulate the funds for such a procedure over time, but my addict mind wants instant gratification. And that's where the problem lies.

Making the Decision and How to Follow Through

I've heard so many excuses why people need to hold on to their credit cards, but I've never, not once, spoken with someone who canceled their cards who regretted doing so. The mythical emergency is just another way to keep you stuck and frightened.

So, I urge you to consider, just to consider, closing your credit cards, lines of credit, overdraft accounts, and any other unsecured sources of credit. But again, you can do this in a balanced way so as not to overwhelm yourself. Maybe just close one a week.

Now, when you call to close your account, you'll likely get push-back from the friendly-sounding representative on the phone. They'll ask you all manner of personal questions or even offer you some type of incentive in order to convince you to keep on debting. They'll not only ask why you want to close the account, they may even ask you inappropriate questions about your debting behavior, such as whether you are in credit counseling. I hope you recognize this for what it is - a shameless intimidation tactic designed to remove *your* freedom of choice. But you don't have to answer any of their questions. You can just keep saying that you want to close the account.

I've experienced similar behavior in stores, where they try to push a store credit card on me just as I'm having my purchases rung up. They'll dangle the great savings I'll get on this purchase. When I say no, I don't debt, they come back by saying that I can go home and cancel the account or I can just pay off the total. Pushing back only makes them dig in deeper because they probably get a bonus for each account they generate. I used to feel ashamed. Now, I simply look them in the eye and tell them I'm a recovering compulsive spender and I live within my means. That usually shuts them up.

What I suggest is that you write yourself a script that anticipates the questions the creditor may ask when you call to cancel. Don't forget, they have no power over you and you don't have to answer their questions. There is no shame in what you are doing. Just the opposite! You are one of the rare few who are serious about living within your means. And that is to be applauded.

I know this may seem scary to deal with, but you can do it. Remember, it's not enough to just cut up the cards. I would do that, and then, scramble to find the number when some bright and shiny object came into view. Or I'd call the credit card company to send me a new card. So, you have to actually close the accounts. And then, take the next step to get the help and support you need to recover from this devastating addiction.

• LESSON #21 •

Quick Tips Regarding Refunds and Library Books

WHEN YOU DECIDE TO LIVE within your means, there are sneaky ways that debting can worm its way into your life. It's a good practice to consider tactics to prevent this from happening.

So, when you get a refund, if you get a store credit or cash in hand, there's no problem spending the money. But if the refund is being credited to your debit card or checking account, I suggest you make it a practice to wait until the refund has cleared your bank account before spending that money. That's because when you are committed to living within your means, you only spend money you actually have. Until it shows up in your bank account, you don't really have it. I can't tell you how many times a refund has not arrived for days or sometimes, it was mistakenly not put back on the card at all, and I had to contact them to ensure it was done.

It's also good practice to allocate the refund back to the category from which you originally spent it whenever possible.

Now, about library books, I'm a big advocate of using the library. It feeds my addiction to acquire books without costing me a penny. However, the vagueness inherent in compulsive spenders means that we have trouble keeping track of when library books are due. And then, you are spending money needlessly for fines. I know it's a minute amount, but it's all part of a pattern of learning to live responsibly.

The best thing is to figure out a system to track when the books are due. I use Google Calendar and when I bring the books home, it would be simple to just note that they are due the week before they're actually due as a reminder.

If you just can't do that, then I suggest creating a category for library book fees, and fund it with $5 or so. But I hope you will begin to realize how senseless it is to pay fines when you can just as easily figure out a way to keep from doing so.

• LESSON #22 •

Checking Accounts with Interest!

THIS IS A WONDERFUL LITTLE secret that has really been a blessing to my husband and I for years!

There are a number of banks that offer interest bearing checking accounts with no minimums and no fees! For the past few years, the interest has been 2.5% or 3%! There is a maximum on which you'll receive the interest, like $10,000 or $15,000, but that's a good problem if you have more money, isn't it? On the last day of the month, the interest you've earned appears in the account. I just love it!

Plus, a number of banks offering this option allow you to open an account even if you don't live in the state where the bank is located! But you do have to use the debit card a certain number of times a month, usually 10 or 12 times. But I use them for all my spending anyway. And you must either have a direct deposit (like your paycheck), or a transfer from another bank account, into their bank. There are some nuances in how to use them, but those are the basics.

You do have to carefully follow their rules or you won't get the interest that month. For instance, I discovered the hard way that Amazon purchases didn't count until I changed how they would be processed (it needed to be entered in as a debit card, not a credit card). Same issue happened with PayPal. So, just ask questions if you aren't sure.

Here are some banks that we've used that provide this service (see resources handout for links):
- Kasasa: an organization that provides these services through member banks
- Lake Michigan Credit Union
- Consumers Credit Union
- Mainstreet Bank

Finally, you can do a Google search for "high interest checking accounts no fees." This program is made for people like us, people who may not have a lot of money, so we can earn a decent interest rate.

• LESSON #23 •

Overview of My Spending Plan Process

I HAVE MADE A VIDEO of my entire spending plan process, which is in this lesson and on my YouTube channel. But I wanted to also give you an overview in this lesson. Here are the basics of what I do:

1. In the morning, I write down what I actually spent yesterday and what I plan to spend today.
2. As I go through my day, if I find the need to spend additional money, I first ensure I have the money available in the associated category. If it is something I need, like gas or a prescription, I go ahead. And if it's something discretionary that can wait, I generally choose to wait until the next morning when I do my daily commitment ... even if I WANT it really, really badly. It's part of exercising the muscle of delayed gratification. This practice is crucial to my continued recovery from compulsive spending. Each time I don't give in, even when I want to, I'm impressing on a deep level that I am able to make a different choice.
3. When I am out and make purchases, I keep the receipts in my wallet. Others may use an app on their phone or write in a notebook.
4. The next morning, I write down all my purchases in my composition book next to the amounts I planned to spend and total them up. And, again, I write down today's planned spending.
5. Pretty much every other day, I also enter my spending into YNAB. Once I have done that, I put a check mark next to the transaction in my composition book to show I've done this.
6. Then, I reconcile with my checking accounts. I have three checking accounts, but two are most active.
7. Once a month, on average, I also reconcile my cash.

8. Once a year, I generate reports about my tax-deductible spending for income tax reporting.

And that's it. Well, there are a few extra steps I do as part of my recovery commitment, but didn't want to complicate the process. Feel free to email me if you'd like to know more. My daily process takes just a few minutes. And living within my means in clarity gives me a lot more time to enjoy my life and freedom from worry around my spending.

• LESSON #24 •

Congratulations and Thank You

YOU HAVE NOW COMPLETED THE Fearless Budgeting "Working with Your Spending Plan" course. If you have done the course work, you will now have a working spending plan. It's up to you what you do with it ongoing. But I hope you will take all you've learned to heart and step into the light of living within your means. If you commit to keeping your numbers and reconciling with your bank account on a regular basis, this habit will only take minutes a day, but will provide you with enormous benefits.

Thank you for trusting me to help you with this process. If you need additional help, you can always email me or leave a question in the student discussion forum.

If you haven't already done so, please consider signing up for email updates, where I will let you know about additional support options, such as "open office hours" where you can join in a conference call to get more personalized help.

Don't forget to check out the "Getting Out from Going Under Daily Reader for Compulsive Debtors and Spenders" and "The Five-Year Recovery Journal." The PDF version of the journal is free to download. (See the resources for links)

And if you have found this course helpful, I'd really appreciate a review. For the online course, just click the button that says, "Rate this course!" in the upper right-hand corner. If you are using the print edition, please consider leaving an Amazon review. Thanks so much for your support.

I wish you all the best on your journey to recovery from compulsive spending and living within your means. I'll end with an analogy I've mentioned before. I see the spending plan as a sword, just like the "sword of truth" that Prince Phillip used to cut through the treacherous and dangerous briars in search of sleeping beauty, and which he used to finally slay the evil fairy Maleficent. My hope is that you embrace your spending plan as your own "sword of truth" to cut through the brambles of addiction to help you find your path of recovery, which you can use to slay your own demons of compulsive spending.

RESOURCES

Download the PDF version of the Resources with clickable links: tinyurl.com/fbworkbook

Resources
Table of Contents

Contact Susan B. 235

Fearless Budgeting Course 236
    Workbooks & Resources Handout 236
    Print and Kindle Version of the Fearless Budgeting Training Course 236
    Downloadable Version of the Fearless Budgeting Training Course 236
    Fearless Budgeting Videos 236

Susan B. Books for Compulsive Spenders 237
    Daily Meditation Book for Compulsive Spenders and Debtors 237
    Five Year Recovery Journal 237

Twelve Step Programs 238
    Pressure Relief Groups 238

Budgeting Software 238

Add Categories and Groups in YNAB 239

Tax Software 239

IRS Income Tax Category Information 239

More Help for Compulsive Spenders from Susan B. 240
    Podcast and Blog 240
    Paying for My Son's College Education ... Hitting My Financial Bottom 240
    My Thoughts on Tithing 240
    Debt Management Company I recommend 240
    Get Your Free Credit Report 240
    Helpful Book to Help with Spending Temptation 240

Wedding Budget Spreadsheet 241

Free Checking Accounts that Pay You Interest 241

Susan B. Artwork 242

Contact Susan B.

Email: fearlessbudgeting@gmail.com
Website: FearlessBudgeting.wordpress.com
Online Training Program Website: fearlessbudgeting.thinkific.com
Note: The Fearless Budgeting Student Discussion Forum is located in the online training program site.

*Sign up for Fearless Budgeting Updates, where you'll be the first to hear about additional support options, such as "Open Office Hours," where you can call into a conference line to ask questions and get more personalized support: tinyurl.com/fbmailinglist.

*NOTE: Long URLS have been shortened using tinyurl.com to make it easier for those reading the print version of the book.

Fearless Budgeting Course

Workbooks & Resources Handout

You can download the following from the Fearless Budgeting online training program and you can also download these files from the following URL: tinyurl.com/fbworkbook.

- **Excel and PDF versions of the workbook** for the Foundational course: "Creating Your Spending Plan" (zipped file)
- **Excel version of the weekly pay worksheet** for course #2: "Working with Your Spending Plan" (.xls format)
- This **resources** handout (.pdf format)
- **Five Year Recovery Journal** by Susan B. (.pdf format)

Print and Kindle Version of the Fearless Budgeting Training Course

The Fearless Budgeting manual is available on Amazon in print and Kindle versions. To read more about the book, go to: FearlessBudgeting.wordpress.com/books

Downloadable Version of the Fearless Budgeting Training Course

The Fearless Budgeting Training Program is offered free online, but you can optionally purchase a downloadable version of the entire audio course (mp3's):
fearlessbudgeting.thinkific.com/courses/paid-option-download-of-entire-fearless-budgeting-course

Fearless Budgeting Videos

You can view all the Fearless Budgeting Videos on my YouTube Channel (tinyurl.com/susanbyoutube). Dealing with Cash in YNAB and my daily process videos are located there as well as in the online course.

Susan B. Books for Compulsive Spenders

Daily Meditation Book for Compulsive Spenders and Debtors

"Getting Out from Going Under Daily Reader for Compulsive Debtors and Spenders" by Susan B. The daily reader offers 366 individual readings. Filled with practical tips, inspiration, and a thought for each day, the *Daily Reader* will encourage and motivate you to stay on the path of recovery.

For more information and to order: tinyurl.com/dailyreadermore

Order on Amazon: tinyurl.com/dailyreaderspenders

Read sample pages: tinyurl.com/dailyreadersamples

Five Year Recovery Journal

"The Five Year Recovery Journal" by Susan B. is a simple and powerful tool to enhance your recovery that will become an invaluable aid to tracking your journey. This 250-page book can be used for all types of addictions and for those who suffer from multiple addictions. It's fun and easy to use. Just one sentence a day, or even a little drawing, will give you a profound picture of your recovery over time.

Download the PDF version for **FREE**! tinyurl.com/fiveyearjournal

Print version available on Amazon: tinyurl.com/amazonjournal

Twelve Step Programs

Debtors Anonymous: debtorsanonymous.org
Underearners Anonymous: underearnersanonymous.org
Spenders Anonymous: spenders.org
Recoveries Anonymous: r-a.org

Pressure Relief Groups

Learn more about Debtors Anonymous (D.A.) pressure relief groups in this blog post from the "Getting Out from Going Under" blog: tinyurl.com/susanbprg

Budgeting Software

TEST YNAB FREE FOR THREE MONTHS!

YNAB® is my preferred budgeting software. It stands for "You Need a Budget." You can read more about YNAB in the Fearless Budgeting Training Program. The reason I recommend YNAB (and no, I don't work for YNAB) is that it's a simple virtual envelope system. It's as close as you can get to keeping track of your money by putting cash in envelopes, which is the cleanest, simplest method for compulsive spenders.

With my affiliate link, you can use YNAB work through the Fearless Budgeting Course #2: "Working with Your Spending Plan" absolutely free! (No payment information required.) The course only takes a week or two. So even if you opt for another alternative and cancel YNAB, you will have a strong grounding in the concepts and practice of working with your spending plan.

Start your FREE three-month trial of YNAB: tinyurl.com/fbynab

For the basics, you can get lots of free training and support from YNAB. They have great tutorials (docs.youneedabudget.com/), an active support forum (support.youneedabudget.com), and free live classes on the basics (youneedabudget.com/classes).

Add Categories and Groups in YNAB

Here is an excellent YNAB support article about how to add categories and groups in YNAB:
docs.youneedabudget.com/article/157-customizing-categories
See the Foundational Course: "Creating Your Spending Plan," lesson #25 ("It's All about Choices") for a couple of step-by-step YNAB tutorials on editing categories.

Tax Software

I use Turbo Tax and find it to be the easiest way for me to do my taxes. It's been invaluable in helping me easily organize my categories for tax deductions. I write about this in the Foundational Course: "Creating Your Spending Plan." You can try TurboTax Free with my affiliate link:
tinyurl.com/fbturbotax

IRS Income Tax Category Information

Here is an IRS publication (PDF) that lists all eligible medical items you can deduct:
irs.gov/pub/irs-pdf/p502.pdf
Beginning on page 5, there is a very simple, easy to read list of items by category that you can deduct. It's not convoluted and complex like most things tax-related.

Here is a link to the user-friendly TurboTax checklist of deductible medical items. Unfortunately, there are plenty of items that you *can't* include as part of your medical deduction:
tinyurl.com/turbomedical

Here are a few more links to help you figure out how to categorize your self-employed expenses and tax deductions:

QuickBooks Complete List of Self-Employed Expenses and Tax Deductions:
quickbooks.intuit.com/r/professional/complete-list-of-self-employed-expenses-and-tax-deductions/

The Balance Small Business: Office Supplies and Office Expenses on Your Business Taxes:
thebalance.com/office-expenses-supplies-taxes-398957

The Balance: Deducting Miscellaneous Business Expenses:
thebalance.com/deducting-miscellaneous-business-expenses-398969

More Help for Compulsive Spenders from Susan B.

Podcast and Blog

PODCAST: "I Can't Stop Spending!" ICantStopSpending.com
BLOG: "Getting Out from Going Under" GettingOutfromGoingUnder.wordpress.com

Paying for My Son's College Education ... Hitting My Financial Bottom

In this article I wrote for The Billfold, you can read about how preparing for my son to go to college caused me to hit my financial bottom in 2009: tinyurl.com/susanbillfold

My Thoughts on Tithing

Here is an episode from the "I Can't Stop Spending!" Podcast all about tithing that I mentioned in lesson #10 of the Foundational course, "Master and Subcategories:" icantstopspending.com/022/

Debt Management Company I recommend

In course #2: "Working with Your Spending Plan, " in lesson #20, "Dealing with Debt," I urged you to listen to this 42-minute podcast of an interview I did with Katie Bossler of Greenpath Financial Wellness (greenpath.com). I think you will find it extremely helpful. It's not just an interview, but an amazing educational seminar that will give you an exceptionally detailed understanding about the different ways debt can be paid off. I learned a lot from this interview – in particular, the difference between a debt management, debt consolidation, and debt settlement program:

icantstopspending.com/026

Get Your Free Credit Report

Here is the link on the Federal Trade Commission (FTC) site to get your free credit report. You could directly access the site they link to, but I thought it was good to send you through the FTC since I know it's legitimate: ftc.gov/faq/consumer-protection/get-my-free-credit-report

Helpful Book to Help with Spending Temptation

I mentioned Claire Weekes' book "Hope and Help for Your Nerves" as a valuable resource in course #2: "Working with Your Spending Plan," lesson #8 "Romancing Temptation:" This is a shortened link that takes you to the book in Amazon (affiliate link): https://amzn.to/2Lp7utg

Wedding Budget Spreadsheet

I talk about this wedding budget spreadsheet in lesson #13 of the Foundational Course. I found a great website is called APracticalWedding.com. Here is a perfect post on that website by Alyssa Griffith called "How to Create a Perfect (For You) Wedding Budget:"

apracticalwedding.com/creative-sample-wedding-budgets

But the coolest part is that she also created a spreadsheet with all the master and subcategories you'd need, along with the percentage of your total budget you'd generally have to spend in each. Here is the link to that fantastic spreadsheet in this lesson as well for you to download:

Shortened link:
tinyurl.com/practicalweddingspreadsheet

Full link:
https://docs.google.com/spreadsheets/d/1XGxcnlTKTQ6bKY_jaj4G6lmr-Nik8ze53KPRhDPOIV_k/edit#gid=0

Free Checking Accounts that Pay You Interest

Read more about this in lesson #22 of the Fearless Budgeting Foundational Course.

There are numerous banks that offer interest bearing checking accounts with no minimums and no fees! There are a few requirements, such as a specific number of debits per month. For the past few years, the interest has been 2.5% or 3%. Here are just a few my husband and I have used.

Kasasa: an organization that provides these services through member banks: kasasa.com/

Lake Michigan Credit Union: lmcu.org/banking/checking/checking_max.aspx

Consumers Credit Union: myconsumers.org/personal/checking/free-rewards-checking

Mainstreet Bank: msbmi.com/personal/checking/kasasa-cash.html

Susan B. Artwork

In lesson #17 of course #2: "Working with Your Spending Plan," I talked about the joy of making gifts and my journey to finding my artistic voice at the age of 55. You can see my art here:

Healingdoodle.pixels.com
Facebook.com/HealingDoodle
Redbubble.com/people/ahealingdoodle
HealingDoodle.com

The "Getting Out from Going Under Daily Reader for Compulsive Debtors and Spenders

The *Getting Out from Going Under Daily Reader for Compulsive Debtors and Spenders*, written by Susan B., a recovering debtor and spender, offers 366 individual readings.

Filled with practical tips, inspiration, and a thought for each day, the *Daily Reader* will encourage and motivate you to stay on the path of recovery. It will be a valuable companion as you work your way through the Fearless Budgeting training program.

The book is available in print and e-book editions on Amazon, Barnes & Noble, Google Play, Apple, and more.

The Amazon print edition is available as a 4"x6" and a larger 5"x8" version.

For more information and to order: tinyurl.com/dailyreadermore

Read sample pages: tinyurl.com/dailyreadersamples

Order on Amazon: https://amzn.to/2KRmJKm (affiliate link)

Listen to the Fearless Budgeting Training Program Online for FREE

OR

Order the Fearless Budgeting Audios

The Fearless Budgeting training program is also offered as a FREE online audio course. You can listen to the audio for each lesson as you read the book to feel even more supported, like talking to a friend on the phone.

Because some people prefer to listen to audios offline, there's also an option to order all 50 mp3 audios in a zipped file.

Check out the online training program and optionally order the training audios: FearlessBudgeting.thinkific.com

Or

Visit the website: FearlessBudgeting.wordpress.com